UNFAIR advantage

THE POWER OF FINANCIAL EDUCATION

WHAT SCHOOLS WILL NEVER TEACH YOU ABOUT MONEY

BY ROBERT T. KIYOSAKI

PLATA
PUBLISHING

Published by Plata Publishing, LLC

CASHFLOW, Rich Dad, Rich Dad's Advisors, ESBI, and B-I Triangle are registered trademarks of CASHFLOW Technologies, Inc.

 are registered trademarks of
CASHFLOW Technologies, Inc.

Plata Publishing, LLC
4330 N. Civic Center Plaza
Suite 100
Scottsdale, AZ 85251
(480) 998-6971

Visit our websites: PlataPublishing.com and RichDad.com

Printed in the United States of America

First Edition: March 2011
ISBN: 978-1-61268-010-1

*This book is dedicated to those who step up
and become part of the solution.*

BESTSELLING BOOKS
BY ROBERT T. KIYOSAKI

Rich Dad Poor Dad
What the Rich Teach Their Kids About Money –
That the Poor and Middle Class Do Not

Rich Dad's CASHFLOW Quadrant
Rich Dad's Guide to Financial Freedom

Rich Dad's Guide to Investing
What the Rich Invest in That the Poor and Middle Class Do Not

Rich Dad's Rich Kid Smart Kid
Give Your Child a Financial Head Start

Rich Dad's Retire Young Retire Rich
How to Get Rich Quickly and Stay Rich Forever

Rich Dad's Prophecy
Why the Biggest Stock Market Crash in History Is Still Coming...
And How You Can Prepare Yourself and Profit from It!

Rich Dad's Success Stories
Real-Life Success Stories from Real-Life People Who Followed the Rich Dad Lessons

Rich Dad's Guide to Becoming Rich
Without Cutting Up Your Credit Cards
Turn Bad Debt into Good Debt

Rich Dad's Who Took My Money?
Why Slow Investors Lose and Fast Money Wins!

Rich Dad Poor Dad for Teens
The Secrets About Money – That You Don't Learn In School!

Rich Dad's Escape from the Rat Race
How to Become a Rich Kid by Following Rich Dad's Advice

Rich Dad's Before You Quit Your Job
Ten Real-Life Lessons Every Entrepreneur Should Know
About Building a Multi-Million-Dollar Business

Rich Dad's Increase Your Financial IQ
Get Smarter with Your Money

Conspiracy of the Rich
The 8 New Rules of Money

CONTENTS

A Message from Robert

It's Not Cool

I thought long and hard about sharing with you our financial success, especially during times like these. I know that millions of people have lost their jobs, their homes, and their businesses. I also know that, in most situations, it is not polite to talk about financial success. Bragging is never cool, especially about money.

Yet, I decided to write about real-life investments. I want you to understand how we gained our financial education, how we use that education, and why it is an unfair advantage, especially in a declining economy. I write not to brag. I write to encourage people to learn, study, practice, and possibly see the world differently. In 2011, there is a lot of money in the world. There are trillions of dollars looking for a home because governments of the world are printing trillions in counterfeit money, aka fiat currency. Governments do not want the world to go into a depression, so they print more funny money. This is why the price of gold and silver go up and why savers are losers.

The problem is that this phony money is in the hands of only a few people. So, the rich get richer, the poor and middle class grow poorer, the economy worsens, and the problem grows bigger.

According to the U.S. Census Bureau, poverty in America increased to nearly 15 percent of the population in September 2010. This means over 4 million people moved from the middle class into poverty, just as Donald Trump and I predicted in our book *Why We Want You To Be Rich*. This is dangerous. This is not healthy.

At the risk of sounding like a braggart, I decided to write this book about real-life investments. I believe it is uncool to know something and not share what I know. That would be greedy. I write because I believe we need real financial education before the world economy can truly recover. Ultimately, I write because I believe it is better to *teach* people to fish than to *give* people fish.

Robert Kiyosaki

*My rich dad said,
"Choose your teachers wisely."*

HOW DO YOU CATCH A MONKEY?

Natives of Africa and Asia have used this technique to catch monkeys for thousands of years: The hunter finds a tree with a small hole in the tree trunk and places fruits or nuts inside the hole. A monkey comes along, puts their fist in the hole and grabs onto the fruit or the nuts. The monkey's fist, now clenched and filled with the fruit or nuts, cannot be withdrawn from the hole, trapping the monkey. Rather than let go of the fruits or nuts, the monkey twists and turns, pulls and tugs, but refuses to let go. The native returns, and at their leisure, kills or captures the monkey.

Humans are similar to monkeys. Rather than cling to fruits or nuts, humans cling to job security, their possessions, and money. Due to a lack of financial education, like the trapped monkey, most people will spend their lives as wage slaves of their employers and tax slaves of the government.

When the global financial crisis began in 2007, many people clung even more tightly to their jobs in the hope of not being one of those who were laid off. Millions held on tightly to their homes, even though they could not pay the mortgage. Most cut back on their spending and saved more, even though the federal government was printing trillions of dollars, destroying the purchasing power of their savings. Workers stuffed even more money into their retirement plans, even though the stock market had crashed, wiping out their prior gains. And school enrollments boomed, as more people headed back to school, even though unemployment was soaring.

Most People Do Not Know What to Do

By 2010, most people knew there was a global financial crisis. Unfortunately, most people do not know what to do about it. Rather than let go, most people clench their fists tighter and wait for the crisis to pass, praying that their political leaders can solve this global crisis and that happy days will return.

A few know they must make changes. Yet without a strong financial education, they do not know what to do or how to change.

A Decade of Crisis

The problem is that the coming decade, the years from 2010 to 2020, will prove to be the most volatile world-changing decade in world history.

Unfortunately, the people clinging to the relics of the past—relics such as job security, savings, a home, and a retirement plan — will be those who are most ravaged by the global financial storm approaching. I can make this statement with certainty for the following five reasons:

1. *It is the end of the Industrial Age.*

The Industrial Age began around 1500 and ended around 2000.

In 1945, at the end of World War II, the United States was the world's most powerful nation, the biggest of the few remaining empires of the Industrial Age.

During the Industrial Age, countries with industrial technology, factories, great schools, and weapons ruled the world.

During the Industrial Age, the auto industry, airline industry, radio and television industry, and the weapons industry dominated the world of business.

During the Industrial Age, a worker could find a high-paying job for life, be protected by a labor union, and receive a retirement paycheck for life.

Financial education was not important in the Industrial Age.

In 1989 the World Wide Web was born. The Industrial Age ended and the Information Age began.

In the coming decade, more jobs will be replaced by technology as our factories are dismantled, shipped, and rebuilt in low-wage countries. The idea of a high-paying job for life and a retirement paycheck for life is an obsolete idea.

Today, the United States is the biggest debtor nation in world history. The United States cannot afford social programs such as Social Security and Medicare.

In the Information Age, the age where job security and a pension for life are not guaranteed, financial education is essential.

Unfortunately, like a monkey with its fist caught in a tree, millions of workers cling to Industrial-Age ideas such as going to school, job security, steady paychecks, medical benefits, early retirement, and government support for life.

In this book, you will find out what kind of education is best for preparing you for the Information Age.

2. ***The rules of money were changed in 1971.***

In 1971, President Nixon took the U.S. dollar off the gold standard, and the rules of money changed.

In 1971, the U.S. dollar stopped being money and became an instrument of debt. After 1971, savers became losers.

Since 1971, the U.S. dollar has lost 95 percent of its purchasing power. It will not take another forty years to lose the remaining 5 percent.

Tragically, like a monkey with a clenched fist in a tree, millions of people still cling tightly to their savings in a bank.

In this book you will find out why saving money is foolish and what you can do instead.

Since the banks can print money, why can't you? You will find out how you can in this book—but it takes financial education.

3. *After 1971, bank bailouts increased in size.*

By 2010, most people were aware of the subprime mess and the trillions in bank bailouts all over the world.

Today, many are angry that the governments bailed out the rich bank owners and passed the bill on to the taxpayers.

Unfortunately, few people are aware that these bailouts have been going on for years and have increased in size since 1971. In the 1980s, the bank bailouts were only in the millions. By the 1990s, the bank bailouts were in the billions. After 2007, the bailouts became international and are now measured in the trillions.

Unfortunately, due to a lack of financial education, most people think debt is bad. Like the monkey, they are hanging onto their dollars and doing their best to get out of debt.

Most people without a sound financial education think debt is bad—and it is if you do not know how to use debt to make you richer.

In this book you will find out how debt makes bankers, and the financially educated, very rich.

4. *Inflation is rising.*

On January 4, 2000, an ounce of gold cost $282.

Ten years later, on December 30, 2010, the same ounce of gold cost $1,405 an ounce.

In the last decade, when measured against gold, the U.S. dollar lost 398 percent of its value.

On January 4, 2000, oil was $25 a barrel.

By December 31, 2010, oil was $91 a barrel.

In 10 years, the price of oil has gone up by 264 percent. Yet the government still claims there is no inflation.

A smart person would ask:

- "What will an ounce of gold cost at the end of the next decade, on December 31, 2020?"

- "How much will a gallon of gasoline cost in 2020?"

- "What will food cost in the next 10 years?"

These are questions most monkeys do not ask. Instead, monkeys go back to school, work harder, pay higher taxes, pay higher prices, do their best to live below their means, and save, save, save.

As you can tell, you should have invested in gold in 2000 when gold was only $273 an ounce. In this book you will learn what to invest in before the thundering herd gets into the market.

In this book you will learn how to predict the future and how to reduce your risk from the changes that are coming.

5. *I see more poor people.*

In the coming decade, the years between 2010 and 2020, the gap between the haves and have-nots will increase. Many in the middle class today will slip into poverty in the next 10 years.

In other words, there will be more poor people, although they live in rich, first-world countries like the United States, England, France, and Japan.

When the governments chose to bail out the owners of the banks, governments chose to spare the rich at the expense of the poor and middle class. In the coming decade, the rich will get richer and the poor and middle class will grow poorer due to taxes and inflation.

The following are events that will make the next decade tougher for those with limited financial education:

- Baby boomers will retire. In the United States alone, there are 78 million baby boomers. It is estimated that 52 percent of baby boomers do not have enough retirement savings or investments to live on. Social Security and Medicare are broke. Financing these programs will require more taxes from generations born after 1964.

- More jobs will be lost. National, state, city, and local governments are short of money. Many are technically bankrupt.

- From 2007 to 2010, most of the job losses were in the private sector, in large corporations and small businesses.

- The next job losses will come from the public sector. Millions of government jobs will be lost in the coming decade.

This means higher taxes, fewer services, and more unemployment.

For example, in January 2011, Camden, New Jersey, *the second most-dangerous city in the United States,* cut its police force by 50 percent. Camden also reduced the number of firefighters and government workers.

Who wants to live in Camden if crime and fire losses increase? What does a loss of government services do to property values?

In spite of rising unemployment and the loss of traditionally safe jobs, like a monkey clinging to his fruits and nuts, people are returning back to school to train for a new job, higher pay, benefits, and a good pension plan.

This book presents you with some new ideas on what types of education will better prepare you for the future.

In 2010, the U.S. debt was $14 trillion. In reality, according to the National Center for Policy Analysis, the United States owes $107 trillion when Social Security and Medicare are added to the bill. This means the United States is bankrupt.

The United States has three basic options. They are:

1. Default on our debts, aka declare bankruptcy. This will change the world economy.

2. Cut spending, increase taxes, and pay bills. This will change the world economy.

3. Print more money, kill the dollar, and pay the bills with counterfeit money. This will change the world economy.

The average person, like the monkey with its fist stuck in a tree, has no idea what is going on with the U.S. dollar or the world economy. All the average person cares about is making enough money to put food on the table and keep a roof over their head.

Like a monkey clinging to what they have, the average person actually believes the money in their grasp is real money. The average voter actually believes their elected officials can solve this global financial crisis. Few people realize the global financial problem is bigger than any one leader or one country.

In this book you will discover how the rules of money are different in the Information Age and how to adapt to the new global rules of money.

In 1972, President Nixon opened the door to China. Today, China is a very poor country rushing to become the world's next superpower.

In the coming decade, China will continue to grow economically but will also grow more unstable as they battle inflation, position for more world political clout, and push for an international reserve currency outside of the U.S. dollar. Additionally, the economic growth will cause trouble internally as the divide between the rich and the poor grows. Their instability will cause financial ripples, economic booms and busts that will be felt throughout the world.

Like most monkeys, the average person can see the trees but not the forest. Americans are probably in a worse condition, however, because they live in a fishbowl where the world looks in at us, but we cannot see the world outside the fishbowl.

In this book you will learn how to think, act, and do business globally. There is a world of opportunity today—but not for those who think only about the tree they are clinging to.

The Most Exciting Decade in History

The next 10 years, the decade from 2010 to 2020, will prove to be the most exciting decade in world history.

The next 10 years will mark the end of the American Empire. The U.S. dollar will prove to be a fraud, and a whole new world economy will emerge. This borderless world, powered by low-cost technology, will unleash the world's genius and reveal the massive ignorance that ran the old world economy.

For those who are financially educated, prepared, flexible, and adaptable, the next 10 years will be the best of times.

For those who are waiting for the happy days of the past to return, the next 10 years will be the worst of times.

Trapped by Going to School

The key to the new world is education. The problem is that the current school system is trapped in the tar pit of the Industrial Age.

In the Information Age, a person's education and lifelong learning is more important than ever before. Unfortunately, going to school alone will not prepare you financially for a rapidly evolving and expanding world. Simply said, schools change too slowly, and the world is changing too rapidly.

In the Industrial Age, all it took to be successful was the following two types of education:

- Academic education: The ability to read, write, and solve basic mathematical problems.
- Professional education: Education to earn money with by being a productive member of society. For example, medical doctors go to medical school, lawyers go to law school, pilots go to flight school, chefs to go cooking school, and so on.

In the Information Age, we need the following three types of education:

- Academic
- Professional
- Financial

The following question thus arises: Why is there not any financial education in schools?

The answer: Humans trap and train monkeys in school.

If a person has a solid financial education, they will not cling so tightly to job security, a steady paycheck, and a pension. If a person knows the tax laws, they will not pay unnecessary taxes. If they understand the banking system, they will not save money. Rather than call their home an asset, they will know that it is a liability. If they understand inflation, they will not try to live below their means. Rather than get out of debt, they will learn how to use debt to gain wealth. And they will not mindlessly turn their money over to Wall Street bankers, financial planners, and real estate agents in the hope of obtaining a secure retirement.

Most importantly, they will question why they are going to school, who their teachers are, and where their education is leading them.

Education Is a Process

In 1973, I returned home from the Vietnam War. I had one year left on my military contract, and I was looking forward to the next direction my life would take.

In 1973, I was 26 years old, a college graduate with two professional licenses: one as a third mate on oil tankers sailing for Standard Oil, and the second as a pilot, flying for the U.S. Marine Corps. Although both professions could be high-paying with job security, I did not want to either sail or fly.

When I asked my poor dad for advice, he recommended that I follow in his footsteps, which would be to go back to school, get my master's degree, get my PhD, and then get a job with the government.

The problem was that in 1973 my dad was 54 years old, the former superintendent of education for the State of Hawaii, a former Republican candidate for lieutenant governor of Hawaii, and unemployed.

My dad was unemployed because he resigned from the superintendent of education position to run on the Republican ticket against his boss, the governor, a Democrat. When Judge Samuel King and my dad lost the gubernatorial election, the governor informed my dad that the price for his lack of loyalty was to never be allowed to work in state government again.

My dad, although highly educated, could not survive in the real world outside of the educational system. Knowing he could not find a paying government job, my dad took his retirement savings, bought an ice cream franchise and lost it all when his ice cream business failed.

In many ways, it was my poor dad who gave me a glimpse of the future, not for his generation, but for mine.

When he recommended that I follow in his footsteps, I knew whose advice I would follow. After leaving my poor dad's home, I drove to Waikiki to my rich dad's office and asked for his advice.

Education Is Very Important

Both dads had tremendous respect for education—but not for the same education.

One of my unfair advantages is to know the differences between different types of education. The following are three concepts that are helpful when considering different types of education:

1. Education is a process.

A person goes to school to go somewhere and become something. For example, I went to flight school to become a pilot.

The problem with traditional education is that traditional education is a process to becoming an employee. That is why most people say, "Go to school to get a job."

Monkeys don't question why they stuck their hands in a hole in a tree. Most people do not question going to school to get a job and become an employee.

An intelligent person would ask, "What if I don't want to be an employee?"

2. *There are four choices in education.*
   My rich dad explained the diagram of the CASHFLOW Quadrant for me. It was his way of giving me choices in my education and what I wanted to be when I grew up.

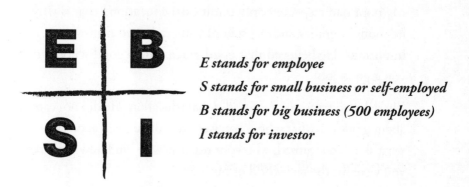

E stands for employee
S stands for small business or self-employed
B stands for big business (500 employees)
I stands for investor

Traditional education prepares students for the E and S quadrants. Examples of S-quadrant schools are law schools, medical schools, and dental schools.

It is interesting that it is the top students from our medical and law schools that pay the most in taxes, and they do so because they are in the S quadrant. To me, if I were a top student, I would want to know how to pay less in taxes. Paying higher taxes is one of the traps of the S quadrant.

When an employee quits their job to start their own business, most wind up in the S quadrant, operating a highly-specialized small business or service business, such as computer consulting or selling real estate.

Like a monkey trapped at one tree, most people only know about the E and S quadrants.

A financially intelligent person would want to know what they have to learn to operate from the B and I quadrants. The B and I quadrants create the richest people in the world, people who earn the most and pay the least in taxes.

In this book you will gain an unfair advantage by understanding what the B and I quadrant people know that E and S quadrant people do not.

3. ***You can choose between traditional or non-traditional education.*** My poor dad respected only traditional education. That is why he thought grades and the school you graduated from were important. He believed that good grades and a good school got you a good job.

My rich dad respected non-traditional education. He did not care about grades or what school you went to. All he cared about was what skills you learned, who your teachers were, and how prepared you were for the real world of business.

My rich dad did not value a high-paying job. Being an entrepreneur, he valued how many high-paying jobs he could create.

That is why in 1973, while still in the Marine Corps, I signed up for non-traditional classes in which I would learn how to:

1. Use debt to invest.
2. Develop sales skills (because "sales equals income").
3. Reduce taxes paid.

Taking the path of non-traditional education in 1973 has given me the biggest unfair advantage in my life.

I continue to take non-traditional educational classes today. Non-traditional education gives me an unfair advantage, even over the smart kids who went to good schools, got good grades, and became well-paid doctors, lawyers, and corporate executives.

Most monkeys do not know the difference between food and food in a trap. That is why they are easily trapped.

A strong financial education teaches students that there are three types of income. They are:

1. Ordinary earned income
2. Portfolio income
3. Passive income

Most E's and S's are trained to work for ordinary earned income. That is why they are so easily trapped, work the hardest, and pay the most in taxes.

In this book you will find out why the financially intelligent work for portfolio, passive, and non-taxable income.

The Difference Between Monkeys and Humans

It may sound cruel to compare human beings to a monkey stuck with its fist in a tree.

I do not do it to be cruel but to make a point. You see, it is cruel to allow Americans to remain financially uneducated, naïvely working hard, paying taxes, and saving money—all the while knowing that something is deeply wrong but not knowing exactly what to do in this period of financial change and uncertainty.

There are similarities between humans and monkeys. For example, a monkey will clench its fist and hang onto fruits and nuts. A human being will hang on tightly to old ideas.

Most of us know this law of physics: Two objects cannot occupy the same space at the same time. For example, you cannot have two cars in a one-car garage. The same is true with thoughts and ideas.

Just as the monkey must let go before it can be free, humans must let go of old ideas before they can be free.

In this book you will learn many unconventional ideas about money and why the rich are getting richer. The main purpose of this book is to present these ideas and challenge any old ideas you might have in place. Then it is up to you to decide if you want to let go of your old ideas and begin to adopt new ideas about money.

Examples of old ideas about money are:

1. **"I'll never be rich."**
   If that idea is not replaced, then the idea becomes your reality. This book was written to change that thought—if you want to change it.

2. **"The rich are greedy."**
   In this book you will find out that being rich requires being generous. You will find that E's and S's are often more greedy than B's and I's.

3. **"I'd rather be happy than rich."**
   Why not be both? Thinking you can only have one is caused by limited thinking.

4. **"Taxes are unfair."**
   In this book you will find that taxes are very fair and how taxes make the financially educated richer.

5. **"I've got to work hard."**
   In this book you will find out why those that work hard pay the most in taxes.

6. **"Investing is risky."**
   In this book you will find out why investing is not risky. Most importantly, you will find out why the financially uneducated are sold the riskiest investments of all.

7. **"Get a good education."**
   In this book you will find out why you need to question where education will take you and who your instructors are.

For example, I enrolled in an MBA program in 1973. My instructors were all employees in the E quadrant. I resigned after six months because I realized that the two-year course of study was programming me to become a well-paid employee in the E quadrant.

If you want to grow into the B and I quadrants, you need instructors and mentors from those quadrants.

In flight school, my first instructors taught me the basics of flying. The next level of instructors taught me advanced flying, which allowed me to graduate from flight school. My next instructors were combat pilots. They were a completely different level of instructor. I already knew how to fly, but the combat-pilot instructors were preparing me for the real world of war.

Financial education is much like flight school. Learning to fly is not a do-it-yourself project. It is best to have the most talented pilots available to educate and train students and give them the opportunity for hands-on experience before they go on to the next level.

One of the problems with traditional education is the absence of real-world experience. Most kids leave school with technical answers to problems but lack the skills needed to put their technical knowledge to good use. This means their most important instructors are the teachers or mentors they meet once they graduate.

One tragedy of this financial crisis is that many college graduates are leaving school but not finding jobs. It is this real-world experience that is crucial to a person's lifelong learning and development and defines who they ultimately become in life.

One reason why so many students leave school and are unable to find a job is that they have been trained to be an employee. They lack the real-life skills to become an entrepreneur.

To make matters worse, many students leave school deeply in debt. Without a job, they cannot pay off their school loans.

School loans are different from home loans. School loans can never be forgiven. This means a person can walk away from a mortgage but not a school loan. If the student cannot find a job, the interest on their school loan accrues unpaid interest. In a few years, the debt explodes due to compounding interest, and the student is trapped like a monkey for life.

8. "I need job security."
In this book you will learn the differences between security and freedom. Security and freedom are exactly opposite. The more security you desire, the less freedom you have. That is why inmates in maximum-security prisons have the least freedom.

Monkeys are trapped because they cling to security.

This book is for those who want freedom and security.

9. "I need to invest for the long term in a well-diversified portfolio of stocks, bonds, and mutual funds."
This could be the worst financial advice of all. Just look at the past decade, often referred to as the "lost decade" for those who invested in stocks, bonds, and mutual funds.

At the start of 2000, the DJIA (Dow Jones Industrial Average) was at 11,357. At the close of 2010, the Dow was 11,577.

Up only a couple hundred points in 10 years. Talk about long-term losers. A 0.2 percent gain in 10 years is a joke, a tragic joke for those who followed this poor advice.

As you already know, gold went from $282 to $1,405 in the same 10 years, a 398 percent gain in 10 years.

If the DJIA had performed as well as gold, in 2010 the DJIA would have been over 45,000.

In spite of these horrible statistics, millions still follow this advice.

Does this mean you should invest in gold?

Absolutely not. This means it is best to gain real-world financial education. If you are like most people and not interested in your financial education, then do as the experts tell you to do, which is to turn your money over to them.

Remember, gold is not a good investment if you are a bad investor. Nothing is a good investment if you are a bad investor.

In this book you will find that the more financial education you have, the more money you make, the less you will pay in taxes, and your returns will go up as your risk goes down.

One day I asked my rich dad, "Do you think real estate is a good investment?"

His reply was, "I don't know. Are you a good investor?"

I then asked, "What advice do you have for the average investor?"

His reply, "Don't be average. Average investors make smart investors rich."

What you invest in—whether it's business, real estate, paper assets, or commodities—is not as important as your investment in yourself. If you are a fool, you will probably lose no matter what you invest in.

This book is about investing in your financial education.

10. "I didn't do well in school. How can I be rich?"
While you do have to go to school to become a doctor or lawyer, you do not have to go to school to be rich or an entrepreneur. Some of the richest people in the world did not graduate from school. Examples are Henry Ford, founder of Ford; Thomas Edison, founder of General Electric; Bill Gates, founder of Microsoft; Mark Zuckerberg, founder of Facebook; Richard Branson, founder of Virgin; Walt Disney, founder of Disney World; and my hero, Steve Jobs, founder of Apple.

Many people are trapped like a monkey today because they went to school and were trained to be workers in the E and S quadrants.

This book is for people who want to know what life is like in the B and I quadrants and what kind of education it takes to get there.

Final Word

On January 24, 2011, on the *Today* show, the following advice from *Consumer Reports* and Jean Chatsky, their resident financial expert, was offered. It is the same advice they been dishing out for years:

1. Live modestly.
2. Have a budget and open a 401(k) retirement plan.
3. Catch up. (In other words, save, save, save.)
4. Pay off debt.
5. Work longer; retire later.

I would never follow this advice. Not only is it bad advice, but it is also depressing advice. Who looks forward to living modestly and saving? On top of being depressing, this advice terrifies me. While this may sound like great advice, especially for the financially uneducated, I believe this is terrible advice.

In this book you will find out why a retirement plan, such as a 401(k), is the worst way to invest. *TIME* magazine in an article entitled "Why It's Time to Retire the 401(k)" in 2009 showed why the 401(k) is a disgrace due to the way it destroys people's wealth.

In the coming decade, the years between 2010 and 2020, the people following this advice from the *Today* show will be hurt the most. They will be whipsawed by ups and downs in the global economy and crushed by higher taxes. They will find life very expensive as inflation goes through the roof. A majority will wind up poorer as their investments in the stock market are lost to market crashes.

The greatest tragedy of all is that people who follow this old advice will miss out on the greatest opportunities in history. Tremendous wealth will be generated in the next 10 years, but not for those following that obsolete advice. Those following the old advice will watch in frustration as the rich become even richer, while life becomes tougher for them.

In chapter one of this book, I go into detail about how the crash that began in 2007 was the best financial opportunity in my lifetime. I expect the next 10 years to be even better.

Time to Let Go

A monkey cannot find freedom until the monkey lets go. The same is true for humans. Humans cannot find freedom until they let go of old, obsolete ideas.

As the old saying goes: The definition of insanity is doing the same thing over and over and expecting a different result. Yet that is what people are doing. They listen to obsolete experts dishing out obsolete financial advice, advice that has not worked. Yet, they continue to cling to those obsolete ideas.

I know it is hard to change old ideas. As they say: You can't teach an old dog new tricks. With humans, it is difficult to change a person who clings tightly to old ideas.

This book is about the unfair advantage a sound financial education can afford anyone, rich or poor, smart or not so smart, living in a rich country or a poor country. With the World Wide Web, anyone living anywhere can gain enormous wealth in the world economy. All they have to do is adopt new ideas, be serious about their financial education, and take action.

Taking action is important because we learn by our mistakes. The idea that mistakes are bad is a bad idea. If people do not make mistakes, they fail to learn, which is why my poor dad remained poor. Rather than look at the loss of his job, the election, and his ice cream business as blessings, he looked at his failures just as a schoolteacher would and punished himself for making mistakes. He died a poor man, not realizing that his failures were his biggest opportunities to learn and to grow.

You see, in school, students who make the most mistakes are labeled stupid. In the real world, people who make the most mistakes and learn from them, become smarter people.

I am happy to report that today I make much more money than my classmates who were the "A" students and became doctors and lawyers. I make more money simply because I made more mistakes and learned from them.

I am not saying this book has the best advice for you. As Warren Buffett says, "Fortunately, there are many ways to financial heaven." I found my way to financial heaven. It is up to you to find your way. This book is merely a guide, not an answer book, because in the real world there are no right answers. There are only answers that work for you.

The primary reason for this book is to offer you new ideas, new ways of looking at the subject of money.

There are many things that I write about that might cause you to say, "This is too good to be true." And they are too good to be true if a person is limited in financial education and real-life experience. Yet for me they are true and can be true for those willing to dedicate more time to their real-life financial education.

Everything in this book is about real life. This book is filled with thoughts, actions, and experiences used every day in my life. This book is about the unfair advantages available to all of us if we are willing to invest in our financial education and learn. I offer these ideas with the intent of challenging old ideas and opening your mind to new ideas.

Remember, you cannot fit two cars in a one-car garage.

Just as a monkey cannot find freedom unless it lets go, human beings cannot change until they let go of old ideas. With the financial challenges up ahead, adopting new ideas is better than clinging to old ideas.

As the Industrial Age and Information Age collide, a massive transfer of wealth is under way. Those who were rich yesterday may not be rich tomorrow. Many who are middle class today, will be poor tomorrow. Just because you were an "A" student yesterday does not mean you know much today.

This book is about letting go of the past and moving into a brave new world of wealth, opportunity, and abundance.

Lessons from Sunday School

I am not very religious, yet I learned very important lessons in Sunday school. Two lessons applicable today are:

1. "Blessed are the meek for they shall inherit the earth."
   The meek does not mean the weak. The meek are those who are humble enough to know they need to reduce their arrogance and be willing to learn anew.
2. "My people perish from a lack of knowledge."

The real financial crisis is a crisis of an educational system that is old, obsolete, and out of touch with the real world. The financial crisis will not go away until our schools inform students about the truths behind jobs, work, taxes, and investing. It is time our schools stop training students to become monkeys with their fist stuck in a tree.

If we don't teach people about money, we will have many more people like my poor dad, a very good, well-educated, hard-working, and honest man, but a man who died angry at the rich and expecting the government to take care of him.

It is time we set people free. Financial education can do that.

Good luck reading this book, and may you gain more knowledge, because knowledge is real money.

Chapter One

UNFAIR ADVANTAGE #1: KNOWLEDGE

What Should I Do with My Money?

FAQ (Frequently Asked Question)

I have $10,000. What should I do with it? What should I invest in?

Short Answer

If you do not know what to do with your money, the best thing to do is not tell anyone.

Explanation

If you do not know what to do with your money, there are many people who will tell you what to do, which is, "Turn your money over to me. I'll take care of it for you."

The biggest losers during the latest financial crisis were people who turned their money over to people they trusted.

Longer Answer

Your level of financial education determines what you do with your money and how you invest.

Explanation

Without financial education, your risks go up, your taxes go up, your returns go down. People without financial education traditionally invest in a home, stocks, bonds, mutual funds, and savings in a bank. These are the riskiest of all investments.

With financial education, your risks go down, returns go up, and taxes go down. In other words, you can make more money with less risk and pay less in taxes. The problem is that you cannot follow traditional financial advice or invest in traditional investments.

What This Book Is About: *With very high-quality financial education,* money flows in rather than out. You can pay zero in taxes and earn millions with very low risk by using other people's money in good or bad economies. This is an extreme unfair advantage.

Who Do You Call for Financial Advice?

In 2007, the world awoke to a new word: subprime. As the financial world began to shake, once-respected financial giants began to wobble. Some collapsed into a pile of rubble.

On September 15, 2008, the Lehman Brothers investment bank declared bankruptcy, the largest bankruptcy filing in U.S. history.

Also in 2008, Merrill Lynch, the largest stock brokerage firm in the United States, went bankrupt and sold itself to Bank of America. The irony is that Merrill Lynch was the firm millions trusted with their wealth, the firm millions looked to for financial advice.

In 2011, all is well at Merrill again. On their website, they promote contacting "a financial advisor to help you rebuild your assets today." Notice the word "rebuild." An intelligent question might be, "Why would anyone have to rebuild?" If you lost money, why would you give them more money?

AIG, Fannie Mae, and Freddie Mac are still in serious trouble. Even Warren Buffett, reportedly the world's richest and smartest investor, and his firm Berkshire Hathaway took substantial losses in the crisis. In fact, it was the Moody's ratings agency, an agency he controls, that issued AAA ratings to subprime mortgages and sold these toxic mortgages, aka derivatives, to governments, pension funds, and investors throughout the world. Selling subprime debt packaged as AAA prime debt is also known as fraud. Buffett's firm was instrumental in triggering this global crisis, yet the world still looks to Warren for fatherly investment advice. On top of that, the companies he controls (Wells Fargo, American Express, General Electric, and Goldman Sachs) received billions in taxpayer bailout money after the crash. Is this Warren Buffett's real secret to being the world's smartest investor?

Also during this crisis, millions of people lost their homes to foreclosures. Millions more are upside down, which means their homes are now worth less than their mortgages.

In 2010, Boston College released a report stating that Americans are $6.6 trillion short in their retirement funds. Their study claims that losses in retirement accounts and home values will leave Americans short of money for retirement. If they cannot afford to retire, what will they do when they can no longer work? Push a shopping cart and live under a bridge? What happens if their health fails? Who takes care of them?

Milliman, Inc., a Seattle-based consulting firm, reported that defined-benefit pension plans of the 100 largest corporations lost $108 billion in August 2010. That is a huge loss in just one month. This means Americans who felt safe because they worked for a company that had a DB plan, a defined-benefit pension plan are in trouble. They might not receive that guaranteed paycheck for life.

Most workers in the United States have a DC plan, a defined-contribution benefit plan, such as the 401(k). A DC plan means that their retirement depends upon how much is contributed to the pension plan. If there is nothing in their plan, they receive nothing. If the plan runs out or is wiped out, again they receive nothing. If the stock market is down, workers with DC plans are in very big trouble. Rather than retirement being a dream, retirement might turn into a nightmare.

CalPERS, the California Public Employee's Retirement System, is an agency of California's government and manages pension and health benefits for more than 1.6 million public employees, retirees, and their families. In other words, there are a lot of people counting on CalPERS for their financial security.

Unfortunately, it has a reputation as the one public pension that lost more money than all the others combined. Some people say it is the most corrupt and inefficient public pension fund in the United States.

In 2010, Stanford University published a warning stating that CalPERs and CalSTRS, the University of California Retirement System, are collectively unfunded by $500 billion dollars and have engaged in overly risky investments.

Half a trillion dollars is quite a shortfall. There goes the myth of obtaining job and retirement security by working for the government.

The Smartest People in the World

You get my point. Unless you have been living under a rock since 2007, I believe you know the story: the story of how the smartest financial brains in the world, the people we look to for financial wisdom, the men and women who went to the best schools in the world, supposedly receiving the best financial education in the world, caused the biggest financial crisis in world history, a crisis some have called the New Depression.

The question that arises is this: If they're so smart, if the leaders of our financial institutions received the best financial education money could buy, why is the world in such a financial crisis? Why are the rich getting richer, the poor getting poorer, and the middle class shrinking? Why are taxes going up and governments going broke? What happened to the jobs? Why are wages going down as inflation goes up? Why are so many baby boomers, people who followed the advice of the best-educated brains in the investment world, now afraid of running out of money during retirement? Why are so many young people, graduating from school under massive debt, unable to find jobs, jobs that can pay off their student loans? The coming crisis will not be the real estate bankruptcies. The next debt crisis will be defaults on student loans.

Could the problem be the poor quality of our leaders' financial education and the lack of financial education of the masses?

What Is Financial Education?

Today, millions of people are finally saying, "We need financial education in our schools." Yet if the brightest minds in the world got the best financial education money can buy, why are we in a massive financial crisis?

A better question is: What is financial education? If schoolteachers do not know what financial education is, how can they teach it? How did the graduates of our best schools—Harvard, Yale, Princeton, Oxford, and Cambridge—guide us into the world's biggest financial crisis? Why is the University of California teacher's retirement plan in trouble? Did those who manage that retirement plan really receive a financial education? Are kids in schools receiving a financial education? Are schools preparing students for the real world of money?

Before describing what I believe financial education is, I need to point out the differences between *education* and *training*.

In 1969, I entered U.S. Navy flight school at Pensacola, Florida. After three years of flight school, I was flying in Vietnam. Looking back upon the experience, I now realize that I was a *well-trained* pilot. I was not a *well-educated* pilot.

I say that I was well trained because I was trained to fly the helicopter gunship. I had no education as to why we were at war in Vietnam. I did not have any geo-political-economic education. I did not know that Vietnam had been at war for over a thousand years. France and the United States were the last in a long line of imperialist countries trying to conquer Vietnam. I did not know that the war I was fighting was their thousand-year war of Independence, as the Revolutionary War was America's fight for independence from England.

All we were told was that we were the good guys and the communists were the bad guys. I did not know what a communist was. All I knew was that we wore white hats and they wore black pajamas. We believed in God and communists did not. I did not know we were fighting for oil and control over the resources of Vietnam and the rest of Southeast Asia. Sadly, I see the same thing going on in Iraq and Afghanistan today.

Also, I had no idea how to design, build, or repair a helicopter. I was not educated in metallurgy, design, electronics, fuel, or weapons systems. I had no idea how to fix my helicopter. All I was trained to do was fly, shoot, and follow orders. Press the right button, and people died. Press the wrong button, and I died. By the end of the war, I was very *well-trained* pilot but not a *well-educated* one.

Potty Training

In the real world, people *toilet train* their children. They do not *toilet educate* their children. People train their dogs. They do not educate their dogs. The term "Pavlov's dog" has come to signify the difference between education and training. In simple terms, ring a bell and Pavlov's dogs salivated and got hungry, even if there was not any food around.

For those not familiar with the term "Pavlov's dog," the term is derived from the famed Russian physiologist and Nobel Laureate Ivan Pavlov (1849–1936), who was recognized for his research on the digestive system of dogs. He is credited with the term "conditioned reflex." Pavlov's dog is used to describe someone who merely reacts to a situation automatically instead of using critical thinking.

Modern advertising uses conditioned reflex extensively. Those of you from my generation may recall that Winston cigarettes had a tag line that went, "Winston tastes good ___ _ _____ ____." At home, we filled in the blanks, "Like a cigarette should." Or "How do you spell relief?" Our answer, "R-O-L-A-I-D-S." Advertisers trained us like Pavlov trained his dogs. Today, Aflac uses a duck to keep them on our minds; Geico insurance uses a green gecko to keep them on our minds. The financial-services industry does the same thing. People work hard for their money and, without thinking, turn their money over to banks and pension funds.

In many schools, school administrators are proud to say they have *financial education* in their schools. In reality, it is *financial training*, not financial education. Just as Pavlov trained his dogs to salivate even if there was nothing to salivate about, millions of highly educated people are *trained* rather than *educated* when it comes to the subject of money. For example, I will give you a test to see if you can fill in the blanks:

- **Go to school, get good grades, and get a _ _ _.**
- **Work _ _ _ _ .**
- **Save _ _ _ _ _ .**
- **Buy a house because your house is an _ _ _ _ _ .**
- **Cut up your credit cards. Get out of _ _ _ _ .**
- **Live _ _ _ _ _ your means.**
- **Invest for the _ _ _ _ term in a well-_ _ _ _ _ _ _ _ _ _ _ _ portfolio of _ _ _ _ _, bonds, and _ _ _ _ _ _ funds.**

Many educated people think this is financial education. On television, it is common to see so-called financial experts saying, "Go to school. Get a job. Save money. Cut up your credit cards, and get out of debt. Your house is an asset. Live below your means. Invest for the long term in a well-diversified portfolio of stocks, bonds, and mutual funds." This is not financial education. This is financial training, the same training that Pavlov used on his dogs and that advertisers use to sell cigarettes, antacids, and insurance.

When the 2007 financial crisis hit, many of those who followed this financial training believed that they were financially educated and lost everything: jobs, homes, retirement, and savings. Many marriages broke apart.

To make matters worse, schools getting on the financial-education bandwagon continue to bring in bankers to promote the wisdom of "saving money." In the name of financial education, schools also bring in financial planners who train young minds to believe that "investing for the long term in a well-diversified portfolio of stocks, bonds, and mutual funds" is the smart thing to do. Mindlessly sending your money to complete strangers is not the end result of good financial education. It is the end result of dog training.

I am certain these educators are well-intentioned people, but their conditioned reflexes blind them to the fact that the bankers and financial planners they invite into their schools work for the very organizations that caused and profited from this financial crisis: corporations such as Bank of America, Merrill Lynch, Goldman Sachs, and Lehman Brothers (oops, they're gone). These companies continue to hire the brightest financially educated students from the best schools in the world and train them to run their companies and sell their financial services. This is not financial education. This is sales training.

Show Me the Money

In 1996, *Jerry McGuire,* a movie starring Renee Zellweger, Tom Cruise, and Cuba Gooding Jr. was released. From that movie came the line, "Show me the money," and today, it is a cult classic. Just a few days ago, I was passing a group of boys between the ages of 10 and 12 who were arguing about money. It seems that one boy owed money to another boy. Frustrated and tired of excuses, the boy who was owed the money stuck out his hand and shouted, "Just show me the money."

What most people think is financial education is really, "Send me your money," not "Show me the money." When a person says, "I have $10,000. What should I do with it?" financial planners, who have very little financial education but lots of sales training, are trained to say, "Invest for the long term in a well-diversified portfolio of stocks, bonds, and mutual funds." In other words, "Send me your money for the long term." People who followed similar mantras are today's biggest losers. This is how Bernie Madoff got so many educated wealthy people to send him billions of dollars, creating the second biggest Ponzi scheme in U.S. history. (The biggest Ponzi scheme in U.S. history is Social Security.)

The term "Ponzi scheme" is named after Charles Ponzi (1882–1949) who was considered one of the greatest swindlers of all time. A Ponzi scheme is an investment fraud where early investors are paid with money coming in from new investors who are generally lured in with the promise of high returns. If you think about it, most markets, real estate, stocks, bonds, and mutual funds are Ponzi schemes. If new investors stop sending in their money in the hopes of higher returns, the scheme collapses.

In 2007, as the news of the subprime crisis spread, old investors and new investors panicked and wanted their money back. Savers also wanted their money back, and the world economy, a massive Ponzi scheme, nearly collapsed. When people stopped sending in their money and began demanding, "Show me my money," the global markets crashed. Millions of ordinary people lost trillions.

To save the world economy, central banks and governments of the world were forced to step in and promise savers and investors that their money was safe. The problem is that millions are still wiped out and millions more do not trust the government and financial systems. They shouldn't. The entire global financial system is a government-sponsored Ponzi scheme. It works as long as you and I keep sending our money to people we hope are trustworthy. Imagine what would happen if young American workers said, "We will not donate any more to Social Security." Not only would the U.S. economy go into chaos but the world economy would probably collapse.

The global Ponzi scheme works for those with financial education and is tragic for those without financial education. This is why I write and teach financial education. The legal, government-sanctioned Ponzi scheme works for me, which is why I do not have a job, save money, call my house an asset, get out of debt, live below my means, or invest for the long term in a diversified portfolio of stocks, bonds, and mutual funds. Unfortunately, the global financial system is corrupt, and millions who follow this advice are being destroyed financially.

The Five Components of Financial Education
To keep financial education as simple as possible, I break it down into five basic components. They are:
- History
- Definitions
- Taxes
- Debt
- Two sides to every coin

Throughout this book, I will often refer to these five basic components of financial education, doing my best to keep things as simple as possible.

Keeping It Simple

Growing up in Hawaii, far from the financial capitals of the world, my financial education began when I was nine years old. My rich dad, my best friend's father, began teaching his son and me about money using the game of *Monopoly.* He kept his lessons very simple.

During one of his lessons, he said, "One of the world's greatest financial strategies is found in the game of *Monopoly.*"

Curious, his son and I asked, "What is the formula?"

Chuckling, he said, "Can't you see it? You've played this game for years. The formula is sitting right in front of you."

The problem is that we could not see it. No matter how many times we went around "GO" and collected our $200, we were blind to what rich dad saw.

Finally rich dad said. "One of the great formulas of the rich is: Four green houses turn into one red hotel."

Later that day, he drove his son and me out to see his real *green houses.* He had about five acres of them. "One day," he said, "I will have my big red hotel." Taking a moment to gather his thoughts, he said, "There are many different formulas. This is the formula I will follow for the rest of my life. I do not have an education. I did not go to school like you boys. Although not formally educated, I will dedicate my life to learning to have this formula work for me."

He kept his word. Rather than go to traditional schools, rich dad often flew from our little town of Hilo, Hawaii, to Honolulu, the capital, on another island, to attend business, sales, and investment courses. His goal was not to get a college degree so he could get a job. He did not want a job. His goal was to get an education that would fuel his plan to great wealth.

Ten years later when I was 19 years old, I returned home from school in New York for Christmas break. For our New Year's celebration, rich dad's son and I had a roaring party in the penthouse of rich dad's real red hotel on the beach at Waikiki. After midnight, when the party was over, I stood on the balcony of his penthouse staring at Waikiki Beach in front of me, realizing rich dad had played *Monopoly* in real life. He had followed his plan. In ten years, I witnessed him going from poor to very rich. By the end of his life, he had five red hotels on different islands and many other properties, businesses, and assets.

Today, when back in Hawaii, I often drive by buildings his family still owns and continues to collect income from, even though rich dad is no longer with us. Even after death, he remained a rich man.

As some of you know, hanging onto your wealth can be as hard as achieving wealth. That is why, before he became wealthy, rich dad also took courses in Honolulu on taxes, probate, and asset protection. When I asked him why, he said, "It does not make sense to work hard and have someone or the government take your money from you. If you are not smart, the government will take most of your hard-earned money after you die. Your stockbroker won't return your money after it's lost in a market crash. If you are not smart, an accident or illness can wipe you out. If you are not smart, a lawsuit can take most of your hard-earned money. Before you make your money, you need to learn how to protect it."

Rich dad never finished high school, yet he never stopped his education.

After Kim and I were married, while we were building our business and our investments, we allocated three to four times a year for business or investment education. The good thing about building a business and working on our investments was that we could apply what we learned immediately. Together, we took classes on advertising, gold, options trading, writing sales letters, foreign-exchange trading, creative financing, foreclosures, and asset protection. Like rich dad, this is how Kim and I gained and continue to increase our financial knowledge. In other words, rich dad did not teach me any specific subject. Instead, he taught me how to learn and what to learn. Today, like rich dad, we study hard so we can play *Monopoly* in real life.

The Value of Financial Education

Kim and I were married in 1986. Like many newly married couples, we did not have much money or credit. Adding to our financial challenges, I was still carrying nearly a million dollars in debt, money owed investors from the crash of my first entrepreneurial venture, the nylon-and-Velcro surfer wallet business.

On October 19, 1987, the Dow Jones Industrial Average fell 508 points, a 22 percent drop.

In 1988, George Herbert Walker Bush was elected president of the United States. That year, the savings-and-loan industry crashed, followed by a real estate market crash. Much like the subprime crisis, the destruction spread across the United States and the world. Millions of people lost their jobs and their homes, and the economy headed into a severe recession.

In 1989, as pessimism spread, I said to Kim, "Now is the time to start investing."

Being newly married, deeply in debt, without traditional jobs, and in the process of building a business, it seemed impossible to find someone who would lend us money to invest. To make matters worse, interest rates for investors were running between 9 percent and 14 percent. We were turned down many, many times. Bankers did not understand why we wanted to be investors in one of the worst economies in decades. Most bankers did not like our explanation that we were playing *Monopoly* in real life.

In spite of the rejection, Kim kept studying, taking classes, reading books, and looking at hundreds of properties. Her goal was to buy two houses per year for ten years, for a total of 20 houses. At first the process was slow, but once she caught on, she achieved her goal of 20 houses in just 18 months. Although she achieved her goal eight years ahead of time, she did not stop investing. She was excited. She was learning more and more with each deal, especially the ones that did not go her way. The more she learned, the more she realized how little she knew. Her desire to learn more drove her on.

By 1994, Kim and I were financially free. We sold our business, and reinvested our gains. We owned over sixty investment properties, each of which sent us a check every month. She was 37, and I was 47.

We were still not rich. All we had was $10,000 a month coming in and $3,000 in expenses going out. Although not rich, we were financially free. As best we could tell, we had cash flow for life.

Pressure Test the Plan

In 1994, we retired early because we wanted to pressure test our retirement plan. We wanted to make sure it could survive in good times and bad times. If our plan did not work, we were still young enough to correct and rebuild our investment base.

Early Retirement Ends

Two years later, bored and tired of retirement, Kim and I got back to work and produced *CASHFLOW,* our financial education game. The game is designed to be a seminar in a box and to teach the financial lessons my rich dad taught me. Like my rich dad, the game does not give you answers. The game challenges you to think. Every time you play the game, the game is different, because the players and challenges are different. The game also comes in three levels: the fundamental version, *CASHFLOW 101;* the advanced version, *CASHFLOW 202;* and *CASHFLOW for Kids,* a version for children 12 and under.

In 2004, the *New York Times* did nearly a full-page article on the game, stating that there were CASHFLOW clubs all over the world with people teaching people the lessons my rich dad taught me. Today, the game is in published in 15 languages. It is also played worldwide via the online versions of the game.

In 1997, *Rich Dad Poor Dad* was published. In the book, I repeated rich dad's lesson, "Your house is not an asset." Howls of protest went up, especially from real estate agents. In 2007, as real estate crashed, millions of people are discovering the value of rich dad's lesson.

In 2000, Oprah called. I appeared on her show and became "an overnight success;" that is, in one night I became famous, but it took me forty years of struggle to truly become successful.

After Oprah, money poured in from books and game sales from

all over the world, but our money formula stayed the same. It was the same "pressure tested" formula that worked in good times and bad, when we had very little money and when we had a lot of money.

In 2002, *Rich Dad's Prophecy* was published. *Prophecy* predicted the biggest stock-market crash in history was coming. The prediction was heresy because the world was in a boom, the biggest bubble in history, a bubble that, as the book predicts, would wipe out the retirement plans of millions of people. Today, that prophecy is coming true.

Rich Dad's Prophecy attracted the attention of Wall Street, and I came under serious attack. I was discredited in the press through *Money* magazine, *Smart Money*, the *Wall Street Journal*, radio, television, and the World Wide Web. I understand. I am a businessman. Wall Street had to protect their cash cow.

In the introduction of *Rich Dad's Prophecy*, I stated, "[Y]ou may have until 2010 to become prepared." In spite of the warning, millions kept betting on the stock market and used their homes as ATMs (automatic teller machines), withdrawing money as the price of real estate went up. The book was actually written in 2001, yet my prediction for 2010 was pretty much on the money. I could not have made this prediction if I had not invested so much time on my financial education.

In 2006, at the height of the real estate boom, I was offered a real estate project for $260 million. The package was made up of five championship golf courses and a major 400-room luxury resort in Phoenix, Arizona, where we live. I did not buy the project. When I turned the project down, the seller said to me, "You'll be sorry. In ten years, this package will be worth over $400 million."

"I hope you're correct, but the project does not make sense to me." With that, I shut my brief case and left the room.

In 2006, I appeared on many programs, including a news segment with KTLA in Los Angeles, warning people that the market was about to collapse.

In 2006, Donald Trump and I published *Why We Want You to Be Rich*. The book was about the crash that was imminent and why the middle class would be wiped out. We began writing the book in late 2004. Our position was that poverty was about to increase. Millions in the middle class would move down the economic ladder. Given the choice between being rich or poor, we think being rich is better, hence the title of the book. Donald and I want you to be rich.

As you know, the market began to crash in 2007.

In 2008, with Wolf Blitzer sitting in for Larry, I went on CNN's *Larry King Live* and predicted Lehman Brothers would go down.

In 2008, *Conspiracy of the Rich* was released. It was initially launched free as an online book. Writing *Conspiracy* was a trip because the book was being written as the world financial markets were crashing. The book is about the "Federal Reserve Bank," which is not part of the federal government, has no reserves, and is not a bank. The Federal Reserve Bank was founded in 1913 and is the cause of the present financial crisis. *Conspiracy* also explained why this crisis is not just a financial crisis, why it is not an accident, and why it is not a new crisis. It has been brewing for years.

On September 15, 2008, as I predicted on CNN, Lehman Brothers filed for bankruptcy protection, the largest bankruptcy in U.S. history.

In 2009, the same 400-room luxury resort and five golf courses were again offered to us. This time Kim and I bought the package. Rather than pay $260 million, we paid $46 million, using pension-fund money to buy the property. The seller who wanted $260 million was bankrupt. The crash of 2007 made him poorer but was making us even richer. As stated in *Rich Dad's Prophecy,* "[Y]ou may have until 2010 to become prepared." Kim and I were prepared as deals began to float to the surface.

By 2010, a little over 20 years after starting her financial education in 1989, Kim personally had nearly 3,000 rental units. Her income per month is more than most people earn in years.

I continue to focus primarily on businesses, commercial buildings, oil wells, and my gold and silver mines. The mines were purchased in 1997 and 1999 for very little money because gold and silver prices were very low. We got great prices for those mines. After the mines were developed and proven to have large reserves of gold and silver, they were taken public through IPOs (initial public offerings) through the Toronto stock exchange, as prices of gold and silver climbed.

We also drilled for oil when oil prices were really low. Today, good economy or bad economy, people keep using oil, so we were not hurt in the crash. Most of Kim's apartment units are in areas that produce oil, Oklahoma and Texas. As long as people use oil, people have jobs, and her apartments stay full. With their rent money, she buys more apartment houses.

Combined, Kim and I do very well and grow wealthier, even in a bad economy. On top of that, we earn more and pay even less in taxes, often paying zero taxes legally. This is the power of true financial education and the reason for this book. As Donald Trump and I stated in our book, "The middle class is disappearing. Given the choice between being rich or poor, we want you to be rich." That is why financial education is important.

It's Not Cool

As I shared at the beginning of this book, I thought long and hard about sharing with you our financial success, especially during this financial crisis. I know that millions of people have lost their jobs, their homes, and their businesses. I also know that it is not polite to talk about financial success in any situation. Bragging is never cool, especially about money.

Yet I decided to write about real-life investments. I want you to understand how we gained our financial education, how we use our education, and why it is an unfair advantage, especially in a declining economy. I write not to brag. I write to encourage people to learn, study, practice, and possibly see the world differently. There is a lot of money in the world. There are trillions of dollars looking for a home because governments of the world are printing trillions in counterfeit money, aka fiat currency. Governments do not want the world to go into a depression so they print more funny money. This is why the price of gold and silver go up and why savers are losers.

The problem is this phony money is in the hands of only a few people so the rich get richer, the poor and middle class grow poorer, the economy worsens, and the problem grows bigger.

In September 2010, poverty in America increased to nearly 15 percent of the population. This means that in less than a year, over 4 million people moved from the middle class into poverty, just as Donald Trump and I predicted. This is dangerous. This is not healthy.

At the risk of sounding like I was bragging, I decided to write this book about real-life investments. I believe it is uncool to know something and not share what I know. That would be greedy. I write because I believe we need real financial education before the world economy can truly recover. Ultimately, I write because I believe it is better to teach people to fish than to give people fish.

Poverty Sucks

Kim and I know what it feels like to be down and out, without money. Anybody who says, "I'm not interested in money," is a moron. I can say from experience, "Poverty sucks." In 1985, Kim and I were homeless for a short period, living in friends' basements or spare rooms as we built our business. We moved many times. Kim should have left me, yet she pushed on, testing our commitment to achieving a better life together. I know she did not marry me for my money because I did not have any money. Once we began to have success with the process my rich dad taught me, we never stopped. Although the start was painful, the ups and downs of the educational process changed our lives into who we are today. Today we know: "Money does not make us rich. Knowledge does." This is the power of real-life financial education and why knowledge is an unfair advantage.

What Is Unfair?

Since the stock-market crash of 1987, the world's economy has gone through two major boom-and-bust cycles. Each boom and each bust made Kim and me stronger financially. In 1990 the economy was similar to 2010. Bad economies are great times to become rich. In 1990, during a very bad recession, Kim and I began our process of going from poor to rich.

The process has not changed. The only thing that changed is the number of zeros. Kim purchased her first investment property in Portland, Oregon, for $45,000. Again, I remind you, we had zero credit and most banks turned us down since we were self-employed and did not have steady jobs. To make matters worse, I had nearly a million dollars in debt dragging behind me. Interest rates were 9 percent to 14 percent for investors. On top of this, we had zero extra cash since all our extra cash was going into growing our international education company. I taught Kim what I knew about creative financing, and magically she came up with $5,000 to purchase the house (by having the seller help us find the credit for the mortgage). After acquiring the property, she earned $25 a month after all expenses, including the mortgage payment. In 1989, she was on her way. She was not rich, but her financial education had begun. It was no longer intellectual theory. It was real life.

Twenty years later, she and I purchased the $46 million resort with five golf courses, but Kim did most of the work. Again, the process is the same. She did not have the money, but she knew how to raise the money. The only change in the process is the number of zeros: $45,000 vs. $46,000,000. What increased was her financial education. Her real-life financial education was a long-term process of classes, seminars, study, reading, successes, failures, good times, bad times, crooks, con men, liars, cheats, mentors, bad partners, and great partners. As her knowledge increased, her confidence increased, risk went down, and the size of her investments increased. This is her unfair advantage today, and why she is qualified to write her book, *Rich Woman,* to encourage other women to take control of their financial future by gaining real-life financial education.

Why Were We Not Wiped Out?

FAQ

Millions of investors lost everything starting in 2007. How did you gain and not lose?

Short Answer

Financial education gave us the ability to not follow conventional financial wisdom.

FAQ

What did you know that others did not know? Why did you win even as the economy was crashing?

Very Short Answer

We kept playing *Monopoly*.

Explanation

There are three priceless lessons in *Monopoly*. They are:

- **1ˢᵗ Lesson: Four green houses, one red hotel**

  The lesson is: *Start small. Dream big.* We both took classes and did small deals on weekends. We had a rule: We had to look at 100 properties before we bought one. With every deal we looked at, especially the bad ones, we got smarter. As you may know, most investments are bad investments, so you need to invest time looking for those rare great deals.

  It doesn't have to be real estate investing. It could be stocks, or a business. The lesson is that most people, especially men, jump into a market, create a big splash, and try to make a killing. Usually, they are the ones who are killed.

  Give yourself at least five to ten years to learn and gain from experience. If you like real estate, start with real estate. If you like stocks, start with stocks. If you are interested in business, start in business. Know that you will make mistakes, so make small mistakes, learn, and keep dreaming big.

- **2nd Lesson: One house-$10, Two houses-$20, Three houses-$30**
  The lesson is: *cash flow*. More houses—more cash flow.
  Red hotel—extreme cash flow.

In the world of money and financial education, *cash flow is the single most important word.* Cash is always flowing. It is either flowing in, or it is flowing out. For most people, they work hard and the cash flows out. True financial education trains you to have cash flowing in.

Financially educated investors must know the difference between cash flow and capital gains.

Most uneducated investors invest for capital gains. That is why amateurs say such things as:

1. "The value of my house went up."
2. "The price of my stock went up so I sold it."
3. "Do you think investing in the emerging markets is smart?"
4. "I'm investing in gold because the price is going up."
5. "You should rebalance your portfolio."
6. "My net worth has increased."
7. "I invest in antique cars because they increase in value."

Simply put, the people who lost during this financial crisis were people who invest primarily for capital gains. Most of them bet on the price of something going up. When the market crashed, their wealth crashed, and for many, their net worth went negative.

To make things very simple, the diagrams below illustrate the differences between cash flow and capital gains.

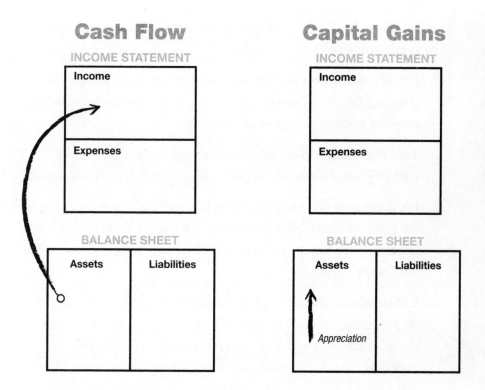

When Kim and I buy a property, we invest primarily for cash flow, diagram #1. We want to see the financial statement. Whether it is a 2-bedroom rental house for $45,000 or a 400-room luxury resort with five golf courses for $46,000,000, investing for cash flow means we must have cash flowing in. When the economy crashed with over 3,000 rental units and commercial properties, cash flow kept pouring in, even as the economy dried up.

Cash kept flowing in because we make sure there are solid jobs in the area before buying anything. Always remember that real estate is only as valuable as the jobs. We did not invest in high-end residential properties. With our partner Ken McElroy, we invested primarily in "workforce housing" properties in areas that need a strong, steady work force.

This is why we have properties in Texas and Oklahoma because oil requires workers. Even in the crash, people still need a roof over their head, and the world kept burning oil. We also invest in workforce housing in college towns because college towns have steady employment.

In real estate, it was the "flippers" who got crushed. Flippers were investing for *capital gains*, diagram #2. They were counting on the property bubble to keep prices rising.

Then they would sell the property to a bigger sucker and make a killing. When the property bubble crashed, the flipper was the sucker.

I'm going to repeat the lesson now because it is worth repeating. In the game of *Monopoly*, the lesson is *cash flow*. Whether it is a green house or a red hotel, cash flows in, which is how you win the game in *Monopoly* and in real life.

Unfortunately, due to a lack of financial education, I estimate that 90 percent of amateur investors invest for capital gains, hoping prices of stocks or real estate or gold and silver go up. That is gambling, but that is what most financial experts recommend that you do. This is why financial planners tell their investors, "On average, the stock market goes up 8 percent per year." Or real estate agents often say, "Your house will go up in value." They focus on capital gains, and not cash flow. You have to be very smart to invest for cash flow.

Fin Ed Tip
Financial education requires a person to understand the definition of words such as *cash flow* and *capital gains*.

In *Rich Dad Poor Dad*, I wrote about *assets* versus *liabilities*. Simply put, assets put money in your pocket (cash flowing in), and liabilities take money from your pocket (cash flowing out). For most people, even if their home has no debt, cash flows out through real estate taxes, repairs, and insurance. The same is true with cars and anything else that sucks cash from your pockets.

On the flip side, most of the properties Kim and I purchase produce income after all expenses and debt. Knowing the difference between cash flow and capital gains gave us an unfair advantage. The reason we look at so many properties is because finding properties that provide cash flow can be daunting. The good news is that finding properties that provide cash flow in a crash is easier, because prices are lower.

The biggest losers during this financial crisis were people who invested in liabilities, hoping for capital gains. When the markets crashed, their cash flowed out.

Average investors invest for capital gains. Capital-gains investors are not really investors. They are traders, buying with the intent of selling for a higher price (or a lower price, in the case of shorting a market). True investors invest for both capital gains and cash flow. True investors also invest for tax breaks, using as much OPM (other people's money) as possible. Knowing how to do this is an unfair advantage.

Below is a diagram showing the differences between *assets* and *liabilities*.

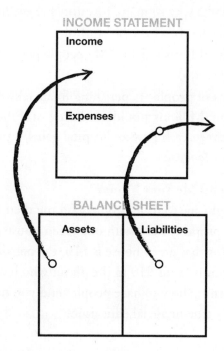

Cash flow is not a goal only in real estate. When I invest in oil, I invest for cash flow. I do not care if the price of oil goes up or down as long as the cash keeps flowing in. Many people invest in stocks for dividends, which is another name for cash flow. Bondholders and savers invest for interest, another name for cash flow. From my books and inventions, I receive royalties, another form of cash flow. Different words—dividends, interest, royalties—yet they all mean the same thing: cash flow.

Unfortunately, after this last crash, dividends and interest from bonds and savings accounts went down. This hurt many retirees counting on that cash flow.

As a kid I learned this priceless lesson from playing *Monopoly*: the lesson of cash flow.

Take a look at the diagram on the preceding page again. Each green house must put money in my pocket, aka cash flow. I never forgot the lesson, and that is why Kim and I did not lose during the 1987 or 2007 financial crashes.

Again, the reason so many millions of people lost trillions is because they invested for capital gains, chart #2. A person who invests for capital gains is gambling, always worried about the ups and downs of the market. That is why so many investors believe investing is risky. Anything is risky when you have no control.

In Sunday school I was taught: "My people perish from a lack of knowledge." (Hosea 4:6)

Today millions of people are perishing financially due to lack of financial education. Millions would not have lost if they simply knew the difference between cash flow and capital gains, a priceless lesson from the game of *Monopoly*.

- **3rd Lesson: Send Me Your Money**

  Monopoly taught me to have people send me their money. When you look at a property deed with one green house on the property and the rent for that green house is $10, the person who lands on that property must send $10 to the player who has the deed to that property. Learning how to have people send you money, as crude as it sounds, is true financial education.

Fin Ed Tip

The financial education taught in schools teaches kids to send their money to the government, retail banks, and investment banks. True financial education teaches you how to have people send money to you.

When the child becomes an adult, this is what their financial statement looks like:

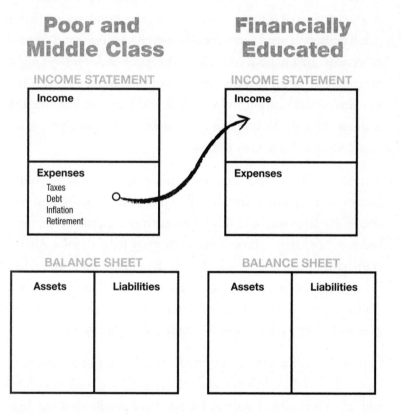

Without financial education, people mindlessly send their money to the government via taxes; to the bank via debt on their house, car, credit cards, and school loans; and to oil companies, power companies, and food producers via inflation. And for those who have a retirement account, they send their money to retail and investment bankers. This is why the rich get richer, the poor stay poor, and the middle class works harder.

Fin Ed Tip

There are two sides to every coin. From the game of *Monopoly*, I learned to be on the receiving end, the other side of the coin. Most people are on the sending side of the coin, and without education, every month their cash flows to those with the most financial education. If you want to be on the receiving side of the coin, your financial education is essential.

At nine years old, I understood the importance of one green house producing $10 of income, positive cash flow. I understood that the rich have people send them their money. Knowing that, I wanted to increase my financial education. The game of *Monopoly* taught me to be one of the persons people send their money to. This is true financial education and why Kim and I did not lose when the markets crashed. We invest in investments that require people to send us money, good economy or bad.

After the market crashed and prices came down, it was the money borrowed from retirement plans that financed our resort and golf course. Banks loaned us millions to buy more apartment houses because they know it is our tenants that pay for the loans. After the crash, consumers still use oil whether the price of oil is up or down. When inflation hits and prices go up, we will still make more money. And as central banks began printing trillions of dollars, the price of gold and silver went up, and we made even more money.

I know this will sound crude, greedy, and vulgar to most people, especially socialists, but the reason I am a lifelong student of financial education is because I want to learn to have people send me their money. Having people sending me money is smarter than being trained like Pavlov's dogs to send more of my hard-earned money to the rich and the government.

As vulgar as learning how to have people send me their money may sound, the truth is that most people only work if the person they work for sends them their money. Even poor people and retirees must wait for the government to send them their money. In other words, the world works only if people send other people money. It's called cash flow. The more important question is whether you want to learn how to have more and more cash flowing in and less and less flowing out. If you do, that requires real financial education.

Kim is a master when it comes to cash flow. She also challenges herself to go beyond what's comfortable for her and has the discipline to achieve the goals she sets and the goals we set as a couple.

Kim's Commentary

My earth-shattering realization came when I realized I had been taught and programmed all my life to focus on the wrong thing when it came to money.

Like probably many of you, I was always told to get a good job, work my way up in the company, and get pay raises along the way. When I was on an hourly pay scale, I was encouraged to work more hours or increase my hourly rate to make more money. This focus of acquiring an ever-increasing salary or income was drummed into me since my first job.

My mind-set shifted when I realized that, in order to become financially independent and free, I needed to focus on acquiring assets, not income. Why? Because focusing on income means *I* have to keep working harder and harder to make more and more money and *maybe* one day I'll have enough money so that I no longer have to work. Shifting my focus to acquiring assets takes the attention off me working forever for money and puts it on my money working forever to make money. This made all the difference.

Every year, Robert and I get together to set our goals. We have our business goals, fitness goals, fun goals, and our asset goals. We want to be sure that each year we add more assets to our asset column. The assets may be businesses, real estate, paper assets, or commodities.

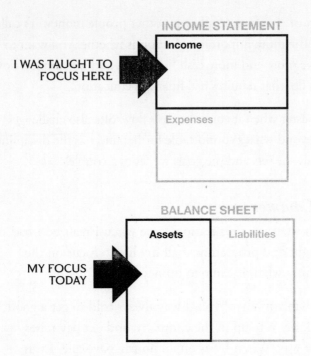

I first started investing in 1989. Fearful and unsure of what I was doing, I stumbled around neighborhoods near our home and finally found a cute 2-bedroom, 1-bath house that seemed to be a good rental prospect. I nervously put in an offer, and with a little back-and-forth negotiation, my offer was accepted. Now more fear kicked in. I was more focused on what I might lose versus what I would get. I looked for every excuse possible for why I shouldn't buy that house. I somehow quieted my fear long enough to go ahead and buy the property, taking very deep breaths along the way.

When all was said and done, I had my very first rental property and a tenant, and once I collected the rent and paid the expenses and the mortgage, I had a massive positive cash flow of $25 per month!

In 1989, after purchasing my small, but charming, rental house, my asset column looked like this:

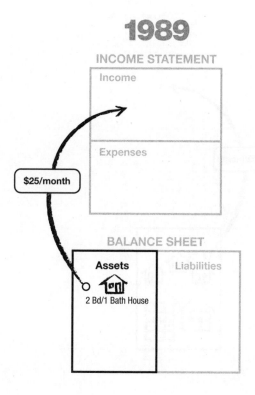

That same year we set our first asset goal. Our goal was to acquire 20 rental units in ten years, or two rentals per year. This was our first smaller goal on the way to our main goal of being financially free. The power of setting the goal is that it is specific and we are crystal-clear on what we want. Setting the goal puts us in motion toward achieving it. The reality is that, once we started toward that goal, my knowledge about real estate investing increased dramatically because I loved it and I was excited about it. I was even more excited about the cash flow that these properties would generate. The fact is that, instead of taking 10 years to reach our goal, we had our 20, actually 21, rental units in 18 months!

Now our asset column looked like this:

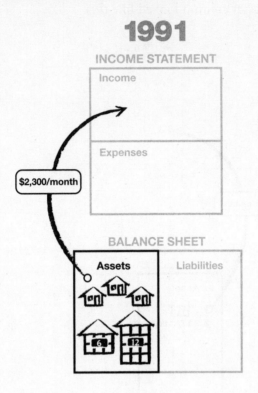

Accomplishing that goal put us much closer to our main goal of being financially free by having the cash flow from our assets greater than our living expenses. This was now our next asset goal: to have more cash flow coming in to us from our assets than was going out in living expenses. It took us three more years to reach that goal.

Here is a snapshot of our asset column in 1994:

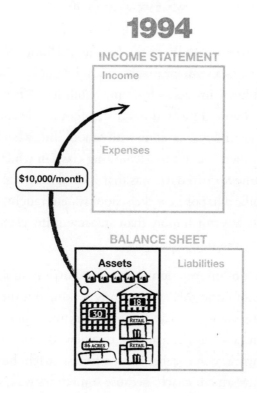

Financial freedom to Robert and me was not amassing millions of dollars in savings on which to live. It was simply to have the cash flow coming in every month from our investments, whether we worked or not. Our cash flow in 1994 was $10,000 per month. This was not mega-dollars, but our expenses at the time were only $3,000 per month. At that point, we were free. Our cash flow from our assets more than paid for our monthly expenses. It was at that moment that we had the luxury to ask ourselves, "What is it we really want to do with our lives?" Being able to ask that question, more than having the money, is true freedom.

As a couple, what is our unfair advantage? First, we set our financial goals *together*. Second, we study and we learn *together* in order to achieve the goals we've set. We attend seminars, read books, meet with real experts, and work with coaches so that we get what we want in life.

My very first gift from Robert when we were first dating was not a nice piece of jewelry or my favorite perfume. No, my first present was a seminar on accounting! I guess he wanted to be sure I knew my assets from my liabilities. When I left college, I vowed I would never step foot inside another classroom again. I was so done with school. But what I discovered when I took this accounting class, in which we played a game for two days, was that I loved learning! I just didn't like what or how the school system taught. So this first gift was much more than an accounting class. It renewed my passion for learning.

There is a lot of information in the world on any subject, especially money, so we are constantly seeking out the most relevant information we can find. At every workshop we attend, I know I will glean at least one new idea that I can apply. We work with coaches, be it a fitness coach, business coach, or investment coach, because sometimes we need that kick in the butt to keep us moving forward.

That is what I see as our unfair advantage. And it's something that anyone can do. It's not rocket science. There is no special sauce. It is, I must say, one of the keys to keeping our relationship new, ever-growing, and fun. And as a couple, it allows us to have what we truly want in our lives.

So every year around New Year's Day, Robert and I set, along with other important goals, our asset goals. The purpose of the goal is to continue to add assets to that all-important column on our financial statements.

Today our asset column is filled with assets from all four of the main asset classes: businesses, real estate, paper assets, and commodities. We've created many businesses that generate cash flow. Our real estate ranges from apartment houses to commercial properties to resorts and golf courses. We have some paper assets in our asset column, and commodities take up a good deal of space in the form of silver, gold, oil, and gas. When the traditional financial advisor recommends you diversify, he or she is usually advising you to diversify within *one* asset class: paper assets. Robert and I diversify, but not within one asset class. We diversify throughout all four asset classes.

It's my experience that what you focus on expands. Setting an asset goal every year and focusing on achieving that goal has definitely expanded our asset column, and yes, it has brought us cash flow. Even more importantly, it has given us freedom.

In Summary

As Kim explained, the true purpose of education is to give a person the power to take information and process it into knowledge.

If a person has no financial education, they cannot process information. They do not know the difference between an asset or a liability, capital gains or cash flow, fundamental investing or technical investing, why the rich pay less in taxes, or why debt makes some people rich and most people poor. They do not know a good investment from a bad investment, or good advice from bad advice. All they know is to go to school, work hard, pay taxes, live below your means, buy a house, get out of debt, and die poor.

As the Bible states, "My people perish from a lack of knowledge." Today, millions are perishing because all they have been *trained* to do is send their money to the rich and to the government. That is not education.

Final Question

FAQ

So what should I invest my money in?

Answer

We all have three choices:

1. Do nothing and *hope* things work out. But as my rich dad said, "Hope is for the hopeless."

2. Turn your money over to an expert for the long term, and "Buy, hold, and pray."

3. Invest in your financial education. Invest your time before you invest your money. That's something you have already done by reading this far. To me, this is the smart thing to do.

Chapter Two
UNFAIR ADVANTAGE #2:
TAXES

Taxes are not fair. Those with financial education can earn more and pay less, even zero taxes, on millions in earnings. Financial knowledge on taxes is an unfair advantage.

FAQ
What do I have to do to earn more money and pay less in taxes?

Short Answer
1. The harder *you work for money*, the more you pay in taxes.
2. The harder *your money works for you*, the less you pay in taxes.
3. The harder *other people's money works for you,* you pay even less in taxes.

You may even pay nothing, zero, zip, nada in taxes. Obviously, this takes the highest levels of financial education. This is a level of education my rich dad inspired me to attain.

Explanation
Many people think taxes are punitive, and for most people they are—simply because most people work for money.

Taxes are also incentives, government-stimulus programs, to encourage people to do what the government wants done. If you do what the government wants, you can earn a lot of money and pay less or even zero in taxes.

The problem is that most people are trained, just as Pavlov trained his dogs, to do what they're told without thinking, namely *to go to school and get a job*. Hence, most people spend their lives working for money and paying more and more taxes.

Simply put, taxes are not fair. For those with the highest of financial education, the more they make, the less they pay in taxes, legally, but only if they do what the government wants them to do.

For most people, taxes make them poorer. Again, they are trained to *send their money to the government*. For a few, taxes make them rich, some very rich. They know how to have *the government send money to them*.

Again, it's about *cash flow*, the most important words in the world of money.

Are the Rules the Same?

FAQ

Is this true just for the United States? Or are taxes the same throughout the world?

Short Answer

Every country has its own tax laws that apply in that country. I am not a tax professional, so I always recommend that people seek professional tax guidance before making any decisions on taxes. To better explain taxes, nationally and internationally, I will have tax expert, Tom Wheelwright, C.P.A., clarify this often-confusing subject.

Professional Answer from Tom Wheelwright

In my study of tax laws around the world, I have found that most countries follow the same basic principles. Tax laws certainly are there to raise revenue for the government. However, they are also used extensively to provide stimulus packages to certain parts of the economy that the government wants to encourage. Similarly, governments throughout the world use tax laws to encourage people to follow the social and energy policies of the government.

FAQ

What is the worst tax advice?

Short Answer

Go to school, get a job, work hard, save money, buy a house because your house is an asset, get out of debt, and invest for the long term in a well-diversified portfolio of stocks, bonds, and mutual funds.

Explanation

Book number two in the Rich Dad series is *Rich Dad's CASHFLOW Quadrant* which defines the different players in the world of money. Pictured below is the CASHFLOW Quadrant:

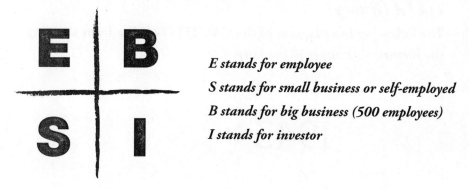

E stands for employee
S stands for small business or self-employed
B stands for big business (500 employees)
I stands for investor

It takes all four quadrants to make the world of money go around.

The quadrants are not professions. For example, a medical doctor can be an E, such as a doctor who works for a B (a big business such as a hospital or drug company). A doctor can also be an S, working as a self-employed, small-business owner in private practice. A doctor can also be a B, the owner of a hospital or a drug company. And the doctor can be an I, an investor.

There is often confusion about the I quadrant. Many people invest their own money in pension or retirement plans by buying and selling stocks and/or mutual funds. That is not the same type of I referred to in the I quadrant. True I's have people *send them money*. Most small investors *send their money* to true I's. Again, the I quadrant is defined by the direction cash is flowing, and that makes a difference in who pays the most in taxes. If you send your money to others to invest for you, you pay more in taxes than the person you send your money to.

My poor dad sent his money to people he trusted to invest for him. My rich dad had people like my poor dad sending money to him.

The difference, from a tax perspective, is like night and day.

FAQ
Which quadrants pay the highest taxes?

Short Answer
The people in the E and S quadrants.

Fin Ed History
The following is a diagram of the CASHFLOW Quadrant showing the historical changes in tax laws:

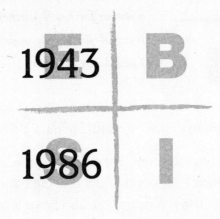

The U.S. Congress passed the "Current Tax Payment Act of 1943" when the United States needed money to fight two wars, one in Europe and one in the Pacific. The 1943 change gave the government the power to force employers to deduct taxes from the employee's paycheck. In other words, the government got paid before the employee got paid. The E quadrant lost control over their money. Today, when employees receive their paycheck, they notice there is a lot of money missing, the difference between net pay and gross pay.

Due to our present financial crisis and the government's need for more money, the gap between gross and net pay is increasing for those in the E quadrant. Employees work harder, earn more, and take home less.

In 1986, Congress passed the "Tax Reform Act of 1986." The purpose of this act was to plug the tax loopholes that people in the S quadrant were enjoying. Up until 1986, most in the S quadrant were using the same tax loopholes the B quadrant enjoyed. Since the government needed more money, they went after the doctors, lawyers, small-business owners, and specialists, such as consultants, real estate brokers, stockbrokers, and other self-employed people.

It was the 1986 Tax Reform Act that helped trigger the 1987 stock-market crash and the 1988 crash of the savings-and-loan industry, which led to the real estate crash, which led to the last recession. It was a great time for B's and I's to get ahead.

Today, doctors, lawyers, and accountants in the S quadrant pay the highest percentages in taxes.

Taxes Are by Quadrant, Not by Profession

It is important to note that taxes are defined by *quadrant,* not by profession. Again, a doctor can be a doctor in all four quadrants. *Different quadrants follow different tax rules.*

When I was in school, I asked a classmate what his father did for a living. His reply was, "My dad is a garbage man."

I did not think much about it until I was invited to his home for Thanksgiving dinner. Rather than pick us up in his car, his dad flew us to their home in his private jet, two hours away from New York. Needless to say, his home was a mansion.

When I inquired about his dad's profession as a garbage man, he said, "My dad owns the largest garbage-collection company in the state. He has over two hundred trucks and over a thousand employees. He also owns the land where the garbage is disposed. His biggest customer is the state and city government."

His dad was a garbage man in the B and I quadrants. He hired garbage men in the E quadrants and uses accountants and attorneys in the S quadrant for specialized advice. If he had good tax advice, paid a much smaller percentage in taxes than his employees.

FAQ

Can a person be in more than one quadrant?

Short Answer

Yes, absolutely. Technically, I am in all four quadrants. I am an E, an employee in my own company. I am an S who writes books and develops games on my own. I am a B with licensed offices all over the world and more than 500 people working to support the business. And I am an I, raising money for my businesses.

FAQ

How does a person change quadrants?

Short Answer

A person begins by deciding to change core values.

Explanation

Again, a medical doctor can be in any or all of the four quadrants. So can you.

Different people seek different quadrants due to core values. I can often tell a person's core values by the words they use. The sections that follow illustrate what I mean.

The E Quadrant
"I want a safe, secure job with benefits."

These are the words of people in the E quadrant. Regardless of whether the person is a janitor or president of the company, they say the same words. These words reflect the core value of *security.* The fear of failing, the need for a steady paycheck, and a fear of change influence their core fears. These people tend to seek long-term careers in the military, the police force, or a big company. If they are ambitious, they may change jobs if a better opportunity to climb the corporate ladder in another company appears, but before they take that leap, they make sure their future paychecks are secure.

Most students in MBA (masters of business administration) programs have dreams of climbing the corporate ladder in the E quadrant, starting near the top. Their MBA gives them an advantage over those who did not get their MBA. A few will make it to the top, becoming president or CEO, and will earn a lot of money. But the problem is that a large percentage of their paycheck will be eaten by taxes.

In the United States, the shining stars of the E quadrant are Jack Welch of General Electric and Meg Whitman of eBay.

FAQ

I am in the E quadrant. What can I do to earn more and pay less in taxes, legally?

Professional Answer from Tom Wheelwright

Not much, so long as you stay in the E quadrant. Most of the tax law is written as a code to reduce taxes for those in the B and the I quadrants. About the best you can do is to postpone taxes through an IRA or 401(k). The real key to reducing taxes is to move into the B and the I quadrants.

The S Quadrant
"If you want it done right, do it yourself."

These are the words of people in the S quadrant, regardless of whether the person is a medical doctor, an attorney, or a yardman. They say the same words. These words reflect the core values of independence and lack of trust that anyone else can do it better. S-quadrant people generally have rigid points of view on the right way, and the wrong way, to do something. Their theme song is: "Nobody Does It Better" or "I Did It My Way." The trouble with the S quadrant is that if they stop working, their income also stops. People in the S quadrant do not own a business. They own a job.

Many professional people fall into the S quadrant. They could be accountants, bookkeepers, webmasters, and consultants. S also stands for specialized or smart. They value their independence and specialized skill. Most stay small because they focus on becoming more specialized, rather than becoming larger.

Shining stars in the S quadrant are often stars in real life. For example, most movie stars, rock stars, and professional athletes are in the S quadrant. In every city and town, there are stars in the S quadrant. For example, there is always the famous local doctor, real estate agent, or restaurant owner in every town.

I have a friend who owns five restaurants in town. He is famous for great Italian food. He earns a lot of money. His kids work in the business, and five restaurants is as big as he wants to get.

Another friend is a famous cancer surgeon. He has people lining up to see him. Since he can only see a few patients, he simply raises his rates. When asked if he wants to grow his business, he says, "I make a lot of money, and I am busy enough."

FAQ

I am in the S quadrant. What can I do to earn more and pay less in taxes, legally?

Professional Answer from Tom Wheelwright

The most important thing to do in an S-quadrant business is to begin thinking and acting like a B-quadrant business. This includes hiring employees, increasing your investment in equipment and real estate and setting up your company as a B-quadrant entity. (An entity is simply your legal form of ownership. Most S-quadrant people are sole proprietorships or partnerships and these entities pay the most tax possible. Instead, look at B-quadrant-type entities such as limited liability companies, limited partnerships, S corporations and C corporations.)

The B Quadrant
"I'm looking for the best people."

These are the words of a B-quadrant person. B means big—500 employees or more. A person in the B quadrant takes on tasks bigger than he or she can do alone. That means success in the B quadrant requires leadership skills and people skills, not just technical skills. This is why so many entrepreneurs, such as Bill Gates, founder of Microsoft; Walt Disney, founder of Disneyland; and Thomas Edison, founder of General Electric did not finish school. Entrepreneurs have the power and leadership skills to take an idea and turn it into a massive business—a business that creates jobs and creates wealth. For example, Silicon Valley in California is wealthy because it is a hotbed for high-tech entrepreneurs.

Success in the B quadrant requires a team effort, because very few people can manage over 500 people on their own.

Shining stars in the B quadrant are Steve Jobs of Apple, Richard Branson of Virgin, and Sergey Brin of Google.

FAQ

I am in the B quadrant. What can I do to earn more and pay less in taxes, legally?

Professional Answer from Tom Wheelwright

The opportunities to reduce taxes in the B quadrant are virtually unlimited. Almost all expenses in a B-quadrant business are deductible. B-quadrant businesses get tax credits for hiring employees, for increasing their research and development, and for investing in green technology. B-quadrant businesses also can often pay taxes at a lower rate than S-quadrant businesses, especially since the owners pay little or no self-employment taxes.

The I Quadrant
"How do I raise the money to invest in my project?
How do I earn more with other people's money and pay less in taxes?"

Earlier I stated that a key distinction of an I is that they use as much OPM as possible.

Shining stars in this quadrant are John Bogle, founder of the Vanguard Funds, and George Soros of Quantum Funds.

FAQ

I am in the I quadrant. What can I do to earn more and pay less in taxes, legally?

Professional Answer from Tom Wheelwright

Using other people's money is literally the best way to reduce your taxes in the I quadrant. That's because you can take deductions for the purchases you make with other people's money. Depreciation on real estate is a particularly great way to take tax benefits on someone else's money. You get a deduction not just for the portion of the real estate you paid for with your own money, but you also get a depreciation deduction for the portion paid for with the bank's money.

The Quadrant in Simple Terms

E's work for someone else.

S's work for themselves.

B's have others work for them.

I's have their money or OPM (other people's money) work for them.

The Bigger Difference

E's and S's work for money, which is why they pay more in taxes.

E's and S's focus here:

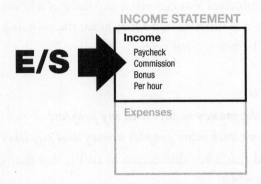

B's and I's work to create or acquire assets, which is why they pay less in taxes. B's and I's focus here:

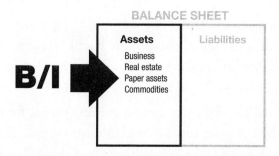

True Capitalist

All the shining stars in the B and I quadrants are capitalists, individuals who took their idea, created a business, and used OPM to grow their business. They spent their time thinking big and focusing on asset creation, which makes it easier to attract capital.

The tough part about being in the S quadrant is that there is very little OPM for growth capital because the entrepreneur's business is small and the S may think too small. There is very little growth potential and too much risk to attract investment capital. That is why most in the S quadrant seek SBA (Small Business Administration) loans that are backed by the government. True capitalists invest in assets, not people.

Most schools do a pretty good job of training students for the E and S quadrants. For example, most universities have MBA programs for students who aspire to be president or CEO of a major corporation, a business that is already built. Most MBA students become employees rather than entrepreneurs because they do not understand the B quadrant. Most recent graduates of MBA programs do not know how to raise capital or how to build assets. The ability to raise capital is the most important skill of an entrepreneur. The inability to raise capital keeps most small businesses small.

Traditional education has great law schools for people who want to be lawyers, and medical schools for those who want to be doctors. There are excellent trade schools training students to be chefs, mechanics, plumbers, auto mechanics, and electricians. The problem with most of these trade schools is that students graduate knowing very little about the B and I quadrants. They graduate knowing very little about money, taxes, debt, investing, raising capital, or how to grow out of the E and S quadrant into the B and I quadrants. If we are to solve the problem of unemployment, we need more people trained and educated to become B's and I's, true capitalists.

The Rich Dad Company focuses on training people for the B and I quadrants. The programs are very different because the people who want to be B's and I's are very different and the skills required to become a B or I are different. Most people who seek paycheck security do not do well in the B or I quadrants, the quadrants with the tax incentives from the government. As Tom Wheelwright explained, these tax incentives exist because governments need more people who know how to create jobs and create excess capital that can be invested in projects of interest to the government, such as housing. Today's unemployment problem is caused by our school system which trains too many students to be employees instead of entrepreneurs, to be workers rather than capitalists.

Changing Quadrants

Before changing quadrants, a person needs to be intimately in touch with their core values, because core values define the person in each of the different quadrants. In other words, you do not change quadrants just for tax reasons.

If you want to change quadrants, take time to define your core values before changing. For example:

- How important is a steady paycheck to you?
- Are you a good leader?
- How do you handle stress?
- Do you have the skills required for the B and I quadrants?
- In which quadrants do you have the greatest chances of success?
- How important is your retirement?

- How do you handle failure?
- Do you work well on teams?
- Do you like your work?
- Is your work getting you to where you want to go in life?

These are important questions that only you can answer. These questions are far more important than taxes.

Simplifying the core values:
E's and S's seek security.
B's and I's seek freedom.

What Should I Change?

FAQ
What is the easiest way to start to change quadrants?

Short Answer
Change your friends.

Explanation
There is a lot of truth to the old saying: Birds of a feather flock together. Employees tend to hang out with employees. Doctors tend to hang out with doctors. The same is true with entrepreneurs and investors. In my experience, people in different quadrants do not like people in other quadrants. That is why labor unions tend to vilify the B and I quadrants, and vice versa. Socialists also tend to distrust people who are in the B and I quadrants, and vice versa. I know that there are some of you reading this section on taxes that vilify me because I have employees and use tax laws to grow richer. I know this to be true because my poor dad truly thought my rich dad was a crook who exploited his employees and cheated on his taxes. My rich dad thought my poor dad was a communist because he belonged to the teachers' union. My poor dad eventually became the leader of the Hawaii State Teachers Union, a promotion that disturbed my rich dad deeply.

As you know, there are crooks and tax cheats in all quadrants. Don't be one of them. It is too easy to have great advisors and play by the rules—the rules of the rich in the B and I quadrants.

Different quadrants attract different people, generally people with the same values and attitudes. People in different quadrants also speak a different dialect, even though it is the same language. For example, employees often say, "I deserve a raise," or "I want more flexible hours." A self-employed person might say, "I can't find good help," or "I'm the best." An entrepreneur in the B quadrant might say, "I need a new president," and "How do we raise the capital to finance the new project?"

One way to meet like-minded people is to attend classes or seminars, join clubs, or simply study and learn a new vocabulary. Soon you will meet new friends.

Exercise: List the six people, outside of work and family, with whom you spend the most time and then determine which quadrant they are in. Since friends are mirrors, this should give you a reflection of yourself.

This does not mean you should dump your old friends, of course. It means you should meet new people and expand your world if you want to change your life.

What Is Wrong with a Job?

FAQ

What is wrong with getting a job, working hard, saving money, buying a house, getting out of debt, and investing for the long term in a well-diversified portfolio of stocks, bonds, and mutual funds?

Short Answer

Taxes.

Longer Answer

The harder you work, the more money you make and the higher percentage you pay in taxes. There is no tax relief for hardworking employees. The primary way to pay less in taxes is to earn less.

If you want to earn more and pay less in taxes, you need to change the type of income you work for.

Explanation

There are three types of taxes for the following three types of income:
1. Earned income (or ordinary income): highest-taxed income
2. Portfolio income: second highest-taxed income
3. Passive income: lowest-taxed income, possibly zero.

Earned Income

People who have a job or are self-employed work for *earned income*. People who save money have their savings work for *earned income*. People who get out of debt pay off their debt with *earned income*. People who buy a house pay for that house with *earned income*. People who have traditional retirement plans, plans such as the 401(k) in America, have their retirement money work for *earned income*.

Get my point? People who follow Pavlov's dog's financial training—getting a job, saving money, buying a house, getting out of debt, and investing in traditional retirement plans—pay the highest taxes, even if it is *their money* that is working for them.

Repeating earlier material in this chapter:
1. The harder *you work for money,* the more you pay in taxes.
2. The harder *your money works for you,* the less you pay in taxes.
3. The harder *other people's money works for you,* the less you pay in taxes. In fact, you may pay nothing, zero, zip, nada, in taxes.

Without financial education, most people work for earned income, and so does their money in savings and traditional retirement plans. They pay the highest taxes possible on their labor and their money.

With a little financial education, at least their money (savings and retirement plan) could work for portfolio or passive income, income that is taxed at lower rates.

Professional Answer from Tom Wheelwright

There is a reason that the tax law rewards those who make their money and other people's money work for them. It's simply because these are the people who invest directly in the economy. The government wants us to invest in the economy to create jobs, housing, and opportunities for others. With a little financial education, anyone can learn how to make the tax laws work in their favor. After all, these are not inadvertent loopholes in the law we are talking about. They are intentional benefits for business owners and investors.

Portfolio Income

Portfolio income is, in most cases, known as capital gains in the investment world. Generally, *capital gains* are achieved when you *buy low* and *sell high*. In the stock market, a person can *sell high and buy low,* aka *shorting* a stock, and achieve capital gains, a profit.

Most people who invest are interested in capital gains. Investing for capital gains is not really investing. It is technically *trading,* which is why it receives a different tax status.

Trading is buying something in order to sell it. Traders do not really want what they have purchased. Traders are no different than a dress-shop owner who buys dresses at wholesale and sells the same dresses at retail. This is why most traders are in the S quadrant, and many are taxed accordingly.

During the real estate bubble, most real estate flippers imagined they were investors. But they were really real estate traders: buying low, sometimes fixing the property up, and selling to a greater fool. These flippers gave true real estate investors a bad name. All these amateurs did was ratchet up prices, muddy the waters, and make a lot of noise about how much money they were making, in the process drawing into the market greater fools than themselves.

The problem was that they were going after capital gains, aka portfolio income, As stated in chapter one, going for capital gains is no different than gambling. At the height of the market, between 2006 and 2007, meek and mild checkout clerks at supermarkets left their timid ways and began flipping properties. Today, we have a crisis simply because people do not know the difference between *capital gains* and *cash flow* (as it is known as in the investment world), or *portfolio income* and *passive income* (as it is known in the accounting world).

Fin Ed Definitions

Investment world		Accounting world
Capital gains	=	*Portfolio income*
Cash flow	=	*Passive income*

Kim and I invest 90 percent of the time for cash flow, aka passive income. When we do invest for capital gains, aka portfolio income, we are extremely cautious, because we know it is gambling.

If you have played our *CASHFLOW* game, you may have noticed that the investment opportunities vary between capital-gains and cash-flow investment deals. A smart investor knows the difference, not only because of risk, but also for taxes.

Very Important Lesson: A person with a high financial IQ knows how to convert different incomes for maximum tax efficiencies. For example, convert earned income into portfolio income and/or passive income. Unfortunately, employees tend to work for earned income and then save for more earned income. They may be highly educated, but they do not know that there are differences in incomes, and they don't know how to convert incomes. Most traders, people who buy and sell stocks or real estate, tend to convert portfolio income into more portfolio income (capital gains) so they never escape the tax rules.

The conversion of income was an important lesson rich dad taught his son and me. That is why his real green houses and real red hotels were important to him. It was through his real estate investments that he converted his earned income into portfolio or passive income. Through his business and investments, he was converting taxable income into non-taxable income. My poor dad, a PhD in education but without financial education, worked harder and harder for taxable income and then saved and invested for more taxable income. He also thought playing *Monopoly* was a waste of time, and that I should be doing my homework so that I could get a good high-paying job and work and save for more earned income.

A subtle, yet important lesson designed into the *CASHFLOW* game is how to convert earned income into portfolio or passive income. The next time you play *CASHFLOW,* notice the conversions of income. Many people miss this important lesson.

Real-Life Investment

In real life, during the insanity of the real estate bubble, we made a lot of money investing for both cash flow and capital gains on one project. The project was approximately 400 units in Scottsdale, Arizona, an affluent city close to Phoenix. At the time, the units were apartments being converted to condominiums. Kim and I took a deep breath, looked at the insanity of the market, and planned our exit strategy: selling 400 condos. (We tend to dislike condos as investments, and so we definitely planned to get rid of them).

We invested with six other investors, $100,000 each, raised a lot of cash via bank loans, converted the apartments to condos with a lot of paint and landscaping, and sold the project out in a year. The real estate market was so hot that people were lining up to buy these well-priced units in a great location.

Kim and I got back our $100,000 and made a little over $1 million in a year. When the project was sold out, and with the assistance of a tax-planning expert, we placed that million into what is known as a 1031 exchange, which means we paid zero taxes and invested the $1 million in capital gains, aka portfolio income, into a

400-unit apartment house in Tucson, Arizona. The million dollars was free money, and tax-free, and today the 400 units produce cash flow, most of which is tax-free because it is passive income coming from real estate.

Technically, Kim and I have a 400-unit apartment house for free, producing passive income every month, tax-free. When the real estate market crashed, we raised rents because more people were renting than buying. Again, we made sure there were stable jobs in the area because real estate is only as valuable as the jobs in the area.

In the next chapter, the chapter on the unfair advantage of debt, I will explain how we got that $1 million back, also tax-free. In other words, our $1 million was returned to Kim and me and was moved into another project. Our entire 400-unit project is completely free, simply because we use debt to get our money back. Even with a free 400-unit apartment house, we receive about $8,000 a month, also almost tax-free. Eight thousand dollars a month is not a lot of money but, without taxes, it is the same as having a job working for $12,000 a month.

Again, please remember that I do not write to brag, because bragging is not cool. I write to explain and inspire some of you to increase your financial education. Also, we did not start at this level. Kim, our partner Ken, and I all started small and dreamed big. Like rich dad, we are always studying, learning, and earning. Financial education and real-life experience is the key. We have no plans on stopping. At this stage in our educational development, why stop? Life is too much fun.

Why Not Stocks, Bonds, or Mutual Funds?

One reason why we usually avoid stocks is because real estate is too easy. On top of that, the tax laws and the use of debt as leverage are different. Another reason that I will get into later in the chapter on risk, is that I have more control over real estate than I do on stocks.

Does this mean you should not invest in paper assets such as stocks, bonds, mutual funds, and ETFs?

The answer is no. If you love paper assets, become the best paper-asset investor you can be. The Rich Dad Company has courses on paper assets because they are an important asset class. The issue with paper assets is control over risk. Once a person knows how to control risk, paper assets can be a fabulous way to secure lifelong wealth.

Personally, I have taken and continue to take classes on paper assets. The reason I take paper-asset classes is because the principles of investing are the same, which means that the principles apply to all assets. It is through classes on paper assets, especially technical analysis and options trading, that I have learned how to be a better businessperson, real estate investor, and predictor of the future.

One disadvantage of paper assets in the United States is tax-deferred capital gains, portfolio income. Years ago, it was possible to 1031-exchange stocks and to defer capital-gains taxes. That tax loophole was closed for paper assets but kept open for U.S. real estate investors.

Professional Answer from Tom Wheelwright

In 1986, when I was working in Washington D.C. in the national tax office of a large accounting firm, Congress decided to change this rule and only allow real estate investors and business owners to avoid taxes through a 1031 exchange. Since then, paper-asset investors do not enjoy the same advantages as real estate investors and business owners. Mutual-fund investors can actually end up paying tax in a year when the mutual fund goes down in value. That's a significant disadvantage to a lack of financial education.

Passive Income

For Kim and me, our objective is always cash flow, aka passive income, which is why we named our game *CASHFLOW*. To us, cash flow for life is our financial freedom. Passive income allowed us to retire early and get on with our lives. Ironically, passive income is also the least taxed of all three incomes.

My book, *Rich Dad Poor Dad,* is about the differences between assets and liabilities. Tragically, most people struggle financially because they refer to liabilities (such as their home, car, boat, and household effects) as "assets." To make matters worse, when they think about investing, they think in terms of capital gains, which is why they think their net worth is important. The problem is that they base their net worth on liabilities, such as their home, car, boat, household goods, and retirement plans. That is why rich dad often said, "Net worth is worth less." Kim and I do not know what our net worth is, but we do know how much cash flow we receive every month.

Keeping definitions simple for two young boys, his son and me, rich dad's definition of an asset is: Assets put money in your pocket, and liabilities take money from your pocket. I came under massive professional attack from so-called highly-educated financial experts for this overly simple definition.

Yet, when you see the world from the viewpoint of an investor and the tax department, you will see the wisdom in the definition's simplicity. If you save money in a bank and invest in a traditional retirement plan, much of your cash will still flow to the tax department. Your tax dollars are passive income for the government. Why not invest in what the government wants you to invest in, and have the government send money to you? To me, that is the smart thing to do.

Kim and I take this to extremes. Since we have excess cash flow, we are always investing, but not in savings, stocks, bonds, mutual funds, or traditional retirement plans. To us, it does not make sense to receive money from the government, and then give it back to the government.

Kim and I do not save money. Since governments of the world are printing trillions of counterfeit dollars, why save dollars? Rather than save money, we save gold and silver inside a self-directed Roth IRA plan because the capital gains from the price of gold and silver going up grows tax-free.

In the following chapter, you will find out how we get the money to invest with. For now, just know that we do not save money for two reasons. Reason number one is, with governments printing money, the value of money has been falling for years. This is also known as inflation. Reason number two is that the interest on savings is taxed at earned-income rates.

Professional Answer from Tom Wheelwright

The tax laws of most developed countries are thousands of pages long. Of all of these pages, only a few are devoted to raising revenue. In fact, in the United States, there really is only one line that raised revenue. It says, effectively, that all income you receive is taxable unless the law says otherwise. And only a few hundred pages tell you how to use a retirement plan to save taxes. Most of the thousands of pages of tax law are devoted to permanently reducing taxes through business and investment deductions, credits, and special tax rates.

FAQ

From a tax point of view, what specifically is wrong with traditional retirement plans like the 401(k) in the United States?

Short Answer

The 401(k) in the United States is designed for people who plan on being poor when they retire. That is why financial planners say, "Your income will go down when you retire." This is their reason for justifying the earned income-tax rate when the person retires. Their financial plan is to plan on earning less when you retire. Because you earn less, you will be in a lower tax bracket. Their plan does not work for someone who plans on being richer when they retire.

Professional Answer from Tom Wheelwright

A traditional retirement plan gives you a deduction for savings today and then taxes you when you retire on everything you pull out of your retirement plan. Sounds good, right? Wrong! For three reasons: First, if you plan to live as well when you retire as you do when you are working, meaning you will actually receive as much income then as you do now, then you will probably be in a higher tax bracket when you retire. This is because you won't have your business deductions, your home mortgage deduction, and deductions for your dependents (hopefully they will be grown and gone).

Second, you could actually be converting passive or portfolio income to ordinary earned income. Consider that if you invest in stocks outside of a retirement plan, you will pay taxes on the gains at the lower capital-gains rates. But if you invest inside a retirement plan, you will pay taxes at the highest ordinary income-tax rates.

Third, and most important, you give up a lot of your control over your money when it's in a retirement plan. You can only invest in certain types of investments (primarily mutual funds), and your employer and the government tell you when you can take the money out and use it.

I used to be like other tax advisors who tell people to max out their retirement funds—that is, until I figured out just how crazy it is to postpone taxes to a year when you are in a higher tax bracket when there are literally thousands of ways to permanently reduce your taxes in the B and I quadrants without ever paying back the government.

FAQ
Is real estate the only asset class with tax advantages?

Short Answer
Governments have many tax-stimulation plans. Kim and I participate only in stimulus projects we know and understand.

Professional Answer from Tom Wheelwright

Most active investments have some sort of stimulus included in the tax law. This includes investments in oil and gas drilling, timber, agriculture, clean energy, and all business. If you really want to know where Congress would like you to put your money, take a look at the tax law. Chances are good that there is a tax break for anything they would like to have you spend money on.

FAQ

What other tax-advantaged investments do you participate in?

Short Answer

Oil and gas wells.

Explanation

In 1966, at the age of 19, I was a junior officer on board Standard Oil tankers sailing up and down the California coast. It was then that I became interested in oil. In the 1970s, I worked for an independent investment banker packaging and selling oil and gas tax shelters to wealthy clients. Today, Kim and I continue to invest in oil and gas projects.

We do not invest in stocks or mutual funds of oil companies such as BP or Exxon. We invest in oil exploration and development partnerships, which means we partner with oil entrepreneurs in specific projects, primarily in Texas, Oklahoma, and Louisiana, coincidently where many of our apartment houses are located. If successful, we receive a percentage of income from the sale of oil and natural gas, aka cash flow with tax advantages.

Oil and natural gas are essential for transportation, food, heating, plastics, and fertilizers. If you look around your kitchen, oil is in use everywhere, even in the foods you eat. The reason the government offers huge tax incentives is because drilling for oil is very risky and oil is essential for life, our economy, and our standard of living.

Real-Life Investment

FAQ

What did you do with the $100,000 you got back from your
400-unit condominium-conversion project in Scottsdale, Arizona?

Short Answer

We invested in an oil-and-gas project in Texas.

Explanation

Again, our objective is cash flow and tax advantages.

The beauty of some oil and gas partnerships is the ROI, return on
investment. The moment Kim and I invested our $100,000 in the
Texas project, we received a 70 percent tax deduction. At my earned
income-tax rate of 40 percent, that is $28,000 cash back. That is a
guaranteed 28 percent ROI in the first year, money the government
technically gives back to me because they want me to invest in oil.

I mention this $28,000 return on my $100,000 investment because
I receive so many calls, especially from stockbrokers saying, "I can get
you a 10 percent return." Why in the world would I want a 10 percent
capital-gains return with so much market risk? I'd rather have a 28
percent guaranteed return from the government in real cash flow, and
not have to gamble on fictitious possible returns on capital gains.

This is what the transaction looks like in a financial statement:

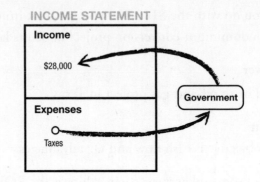

If we strike oil, and that *if* is a real *if*, which is why experience in the oil industry is essential, the financial statement looks like this:

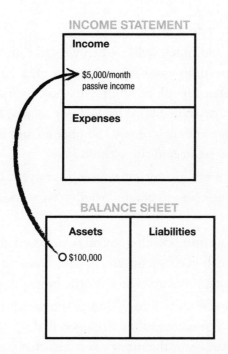

For simplicity, let's say my income from the well is $5,000 a month. (The income will vary with production and oil and gas prices.) The $5,000 in income is also given a tax break of 20 percent, which means I pay tax on $4,000 instead of $5,000. If I earned $5,000 in the E or S quadrants, I would pay tax on the full $5,000.

To me, this type of tax-advantaged investment makes more sense than investing in my 401(k) for forty years, buying, holding, and praying that I have enough money to last the rest of my life.

Ultimate Objectives: Kim and I have the following five objectives:

1. We want our money back. At $5,000 a month or $60,000 a year, plus the $28,000 in tax refunds, we get our $100,000 back in a little more than a year. Try that in a 401(k). If the price of oil is high, as it was when it hit $140 a barrel, we get our money back faster.

2. We move our money into another investment.

3. We want cash flow for life. Wells can last from one year to 60 years. That is why choosing the well and the developer is important before investing.

4. We want additional wells. When we strike oil, there are often more opportunities for oil in the same area. Knowing where to drill reduces our risk of drilling dry holes, which does happen. Drilling a dry hole means we lose our money, but we still get that 28 percent tax write-off. So once an area is proven to be successful, we keep drilling there.

5. We want more income every year. Every year, our cash flow increases at a lower tax rate, whether we work or not.

A Word of Caution: Drilling for oil is an extremely risky venture and that is why such investments are, by law, available only to accredited investors, investors who have the money and knowledge.

The high risk is not in oil itself, but in the entrepreneur who is drilling for oil. Even successful oil drillers drill dry holes. If you do not have the education or the money, it is best that you not invest in oil-drilling partnerships. It is safer for you to invest in shares of oil companies, companies such as BP and Exxon. Shares can be purchased through your stockbroker. Investing in stocks of oil companies, you can achieve capital gains and cash flow from dividends, but you do not receive the tax advantages.

FAQ
What about the environment? What about global warming?

Answer and explanation
I get this question all the time. My reply is, "I too am concerned with the environment." This is why some of the money my investments earn is invested in alternative fuels and power companies. I have a substantial investment in a small start-up solar company. Having seen an atomic bomb go off with my own eyes when I was a kid, I am against nuclear power because nuclear waste stays harmful for thousands of years.

I am confident someone will discover an alternative to fossil and nuclear energy in the next five years. When that happens, the world will be dramatically changed, just as the Internet has dramatically changed the world.

Regardless of your views on oil and the environment, remember that civilization requires energy. We need cheaper, cleaner, alternative energy for civilization to grow. If alternative sources of energy are not developed, civilization goes backwards. This is why I invest in oil and alternative fuels.

Final Comments

Tax is a massive subject. Taxes are also your largest single expense. Due to the current financial crisis, taxes will have to go up. That is why knowledge of taxes is essential to a person's financial education. Remember, tax rules are written for specific quadrants, not professions. This is why the advice, "Go to school to get a job or become a doctor," is bad advice from the tax viewpoint. If a person wants to reduce taxes, they often have to change quadrants or add quadrants.

More important than taxes is your happiness with the quadrant you are in. In other words, changing quadrants just for taxes is not a good idea. If you are happy and successful in the E or S quadrant, stay there and find ways to earn more money, even if you will pay more in taxes.

In the following chapters, I will explain how a person can remain in the E and S quadrants but learn to be an investor in the I quadrant.

Before doing anything with taxes, always seek competent professional tax advice.

In closing, not all tax advisors are equal. Most are in the E and S quadrants and think like accountants in the E and S quadrants. In other words, be careful from whom you get tax advice, even if they are tax accountants or tax attorneys.

An incompetent, lazy, arrogant, or corrupt accountant or attorney can cost you a lot of money. I know from personal experience. Just because someone is an "A" student in school does not mean they are competent or honest in real life.

Professional Answer from Tom Wheelwright

Taxes are a part of life. The simple question is whether you are going to use the tax law to make them a smaller part of your life, or do nothing and let them stay a huge expense. With a sound education on how the tax laws work coupled with better tax planning from a competent tax advisor who understands the laws, most entrepreneurs and investors can permanently reduce their taxes by 10 percent to 40 percent. And the money you save in taxes can be used to invest and build your wealth. So don't wait. Take action now and learn how you can reduce your taxes.

Final Question

FAQ

But what if everyone became B's and I's? Who would pay the taxes?

Short Answer

While possible, it is highly unlikely.

Explanation

It is much easier to be an E or S working, saving, and investing for earned income, the highest taxed of all three incomes.

Chapter Three

UNFAIR ADVANTAGE #3:
DEBT

In 1971, President Richard Nixon took the U.S. dollar off the gold standard. The result: Savers became losers, and debtors became winners.

FAQ

Why did savers become losers?

Short Answer

Because in 1971, the U.S. dollar stopped being real money. And when governments print a lot of funny money, savings lose value.

FAQ

How much money is the U.S. printing?

Short Answer

A lot.

Longer Answer

In 2010, the U.S. national debt was over $13 trillion. Unfunded debt was over $107 trillion and growing.

In 2010, the U.S. government printed nearly $1 billion a day and the amount continues to grow.

How Much Is a Billion?

Let's say a person works for $10 an hour. That means in an eight-hour day, they gross $80.

Most of us know what $80 is, but most of us have no grasp of what $1 billion is. The following conversions might help us get an idea of what a billion is:

1 billion seconds = 31.7 years

1 billion minutes = 1902.5 years

1 billion hours = 114,155 years

1 billion days = 2,739,726 years

1 billion seconds ago was 1979.

1 billion minutes ago was 108 AD

1 billion hours ago was the Stone Age

1 billion days ago humans did not exist

How Much Is a Trillion?

1 trillion seconds = 32,000 years

A trillion is beyond my meager brain. Just multiply the numbers for billions by 1,000 and you will find that a trillion is beyond comprehension. I cannot imagine 32,000 years or one trillion seconds.

FAQ

What does the future look like?

Short Answer

Lots more money being printed.

Explanation

Look at the chart below and you will see how much more money will be printed in the near future.

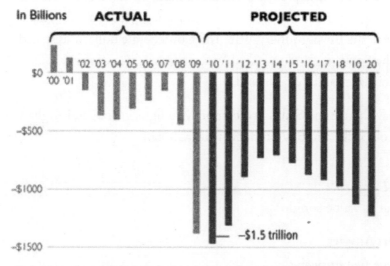

Obama Deficits Will Exceed Previous Deficits

In Billions   **ACTUAL**   **PROJECTED**

Sources: Congressional Budget Office and Office of Management and Budget.

Reprinted with permission   ☎ heritage.org

2010 – U.S. Budget Deficit: $1.5 trillion
2011 – U.S. Budget Deficit: $1.3 trillion

FAQ
What do these numbers mean?

Short Answer
More money will be printed.

FAQ
What does this mean to me?

Short Answer
Higher taxes and inflation.

FAQ
Could the U.S. dollar collapse?

Short Answer

Yes. Currency collapses have occurred many times in America. George Washington issued the Continental currency, paper money used to finance the Revolutionary War. The Confederate dollar was issued by the South to fund the Civil War. These are two of many U.S. currencies that have collapsed.

Today the United States prints money to fight in Iraq and Afghanistan, pay our bills, and buy products from China.

FAQ

What can a person do?

Short Answer

I have two answers:

1. If you have limited financial education, rather than save money, I would save gold and silver. I would buy a little gold and silver with every paycheck and hang on to it. I have been saving gold and silver for years when gold was under $300 an ounce and silver was under $3. I do not save money.

2. If you are financially sophisticated, create your own printing press and print your own money.

FAQ

How do you create your own printing press?

Short Answer

Use debt to acquire assets.

FAQ

Isn't that risky? Is it legal?

Short Answer

It can be risky, but this is what the government wants us to do, which is why it is legal.

In the previous chapter on taxes I wrote:

1. The harder *you work for money*, the more you pay in taxes.
2. The harder *your money works for you*, the less you pay in taxes.
3. The harder *other people's money works for you,* you pay even less in taxes. You may even pay nothing, zero, zip, nada in taxes. Obviously, this takes the highest levels of financial education. This is a level of education my rich dad inspired me to attain.

As strange as it may sound to most people, the government not only wants us to get into debt, the government offers tax incentives to get into debt.

To better understand the relationship between money and debt, a little financial history is important.

Fin Ed History

After 1971, the U.S. printing presses began to run as the government began using counterfeit dollars to pay for its expenses and debt. Because the United States used a lot of oil, U.S. dollars flowed to Saudi Arabia just as oil prices began to rise. As the price for oil rose, more dollars flowed to the Arab world. These petrodollars, as they were called, had to find a home, so these petrodollars flowed to London, because London had banks big enough to handle such a surge in cash. From London, these dollars again needed a home, so the money flowed to anyone who would borrow these petrodollars. Latin American countries gladly borrowed the money and, in the late 1970s and early 1980s, the Latin American economy went into a bubble and burst, causing the Latin American debt crisis. From Latin America, the hot money flowed to Japan, causing a boom and then a bust in 1989. The money then flowed to Mexico, causing the Mexican peso crisis in 1994, the Asian crisis in 1997, and the Russian ruble crisis in 1998.

Arrogantly, American bankers and Wall Street laughed at the rest of the world, since they believed the rolling boom-and-bust bubble would not affect the United States.

During President Clinton's era (1993-2001), the U.S. government balanced its budget, so the United States did not need to borrow any money. This was bad news for the bankers of the world who then needed to find more borrowers, borrowers who could borrow trillions of dollars. They found big borrowers in Fannie Mae and Freddie Mac, which are GSEs, Government-Sponsored Enterprises, U.S. quasi-government agencies that were anxious to borrow money. They borrowed $3 to $5 trillion of this hot money and loaned the money out to almost anyone to buy a new home or refinance their home. The real estate bubble in the United States had begun.

When Fannie Mae and Freddie Mac and their executives came under investigation, they stopped borrowing this hot money. Again, this ocean of counterfeit dollars had to find a home. In the late 1990s, government officials such as Clinton and Fed Chairman Alan Greenspan changed the rules for the biggest banks, such as Goldman Sachs, Bank of America, and Citigroup, which began taking in this money. Immediately these banks needed to find someone to take this money off their hands. As you know, cash must keep flowing.

To help the banks and Wall Street move this hot money, mortgage brokers working for companies such as Countrywide Mortgage started looking for anyone who wanted to borrow money. They went into the poorest neighborhoods in the United States. Millions who did not have jobs or credit were offered "NINJA" (No Income, No Job or Asset) loans, and soon they too were living the American dream. Unfortunately for many, it was a dream they could not afford. The subprime mortgage bubble grew into a massive balloon.

Once these subprime mortgages were processed, the big banks and Wall Street packaged this toxic debt and sold the debt as assets. These new tranches of debt, aka a pile of debt, were called MBSs (Mortgage Backed Securities) and CDOs (Collateralized Debt Obligations), aka derivatives of subprime debt packaged as prime. The biggest banks and Wall Street sold this toxic debt as assets to other banks, pension funds, and investors all over the world. It was not much different than taking horse manure, deodorizing it, putting it in a plastic bag, and selling it as fertilizer. The only difference between a subprime loan and horse manure is that horse manure, used properly, has real value.

In chapter one, I wrote that the people with the best financial education in the world are the people who profited from this crisis. They may not have caused the crisis, but they went along with it. Many made millions and a few made billions. They are still at work shoveling horse manure—or buying it. Can't they smell it? And how could Warren Buffett's rating company, Moody's, bless this horse manure as AAA?

As the smartest guys in the world began spreading this financial horse manure all over the world, global home prices climbed and millions of people all over the world felt rich. They felt rich due to the wealth effect, which means they felt wealthy because their home had gone up in value—again, they were focusing on capital gains. With an increase in home value, millions mistakenly thought their net worth had gone up. With this feeling of euphoria, they began spending, charging like mad bulls with credit cards, paying off their credit cards by refinancing their homes, and blowing the bubble into a giant hot-air balloon. What makes me sick is that these experts, such as former Fed Chairman Greenspan and current Fed Chairman Bernanke, claim not to have seen the biggest hot-air balloon in history.

The following are some of Bernanke's comments as the balloon began to burst:

October 20, 2005: "House prices have risen by nearly 25 percent over the past two years. Although speculative activity has increased in some areas, at a national level these price increases largely reflect strong economic fundamentals."

November 15, 2005: "With respect to their safety, derivatives, for the most part, are traded among very sophisticated institutions and individuals who have considerable incentive to understand them and to use them properly. The Federal Reserve's responsibility is to make sure that the institutions it regulates have good systems and good procedures for ensuring that their derivative portfolios are well-managed and do not create risk in their institutions."

March 28, 2007: "At this juncture, however, the impact on the broader economy and financial markets of the problems in the subprime market seems likely to be contained. In particular, mortgages to prime borrowers and fixed-rate mortgages to all classes of borrowers continue to perform well, with low rates of delinquency."

January 10, 2008: "The Federal Reserve is not currently forecasting a recession."

March 16, 2009: "We'll see the recession coming to an end probably this year."

Mr. Bernanke is a graduate of MIT, a professor at Stanford and Princeton, and may be a brilliant economist. Yet it seems he does not live in the same world as you and I live in.

In 2002, *Rich Dad's Prophecy* was published, predicting that the biggest stock-market crash in history was coming. You do not have to go to MIT, Stanford, or Princeton to see the future. I wrote in the introduction of *Prophecy:* "[Y]ou may have up to the year 2010 to become prepared."

As expected, *Rich Dad's Prophecy* was trashed by leading financial publications such as the *Wall Street Journal* and *Smart Money* magazine.

In 2007, the real estate market began to wobble as subprime borrowers could not make their mortgage payments. A global banking crisis followed, eventually bringing down the United States and Europe with it. After the United States crashed, the European PIIGS—Portugal, Ireland, Italy, Greece, and Spain—collapsed under mountains of debt. If not for Germany, Europe and the euro might have gone down. The debt crisis was solved by creating more debt. The rolling booms and busts that started after 1971 with Arab petrodollars continue. Hot money looks for people and institutions that can borrow more and more money. Ever since 1971, the world economy cannot grow unless people borrow money.

Today there are trillions of dollars (and other fiat currencies) looking for a home, which is why interest rates for borrowers are low and interest rates for savers are also low. Simply put, the financial world loves debtors and punishes savers.

Why Bankers Do Not Like Savers

To better understand the entire global financial crisis, all one needs to do is understand the business of bankers. Pictured below are the financial statements of a banker and a saver:

Banker		Saver	
INCOME STATEMENT		**INCOME STATEMENT**	
Income		Income	
Expenses		Expenses	
BALANCE SHEET		**BALANCE SHEET**	
Assets	**Liabilities** $100	**Assets** $100	Liabilities

Explanation

For the saver, their $100 is an asset. For the banker, the saver's same $100 is a liability.

FAQ

Why is it a liability to the banker?

Short Answer

The definition of an asset is something that puts money in your pocket. The definition of a liability is something that takes money from your pocket. Since the banker must pay interest to the saver, the saver's $100 is the saver's asset and the banker's liability.

Follow arrows and notice direction of cash flowing:

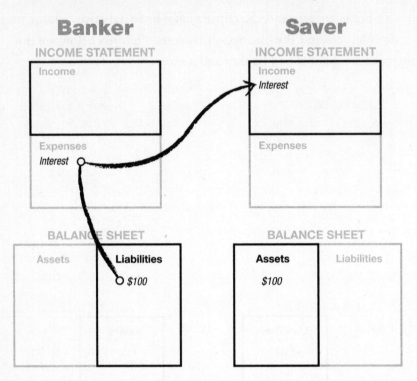

FAQ

How does the banker make money?

Short Answer

Debtors.

Explanation

The banking system of the world works on a system known as the fractional reserve system.

Simply put, for every dollar you save, the bank can lend out a specific multiple of your dollars. For example, let's say you save $1 with a fractional reserve of 10. The banker can lend out $10. Like magic, your $1 becomes $10, which the banker lends out at high interest rates, especially on credit cards. This is how the banks make money from debtors and loses money from savers and why bankers love debtors—the bigger the better.

If the government wants to increase the money supply, the fractional reserve is raised to, let's say, 40, which is what the SEC (Securities and Exchange Commission allowed the biggest five banks to do in order to save the economy in 2004. This 1:40 fractional reserve caused a massive bubble and today we are in a global crisis of debt, debt that cannot be repaid.

When debtors could not repay their loans, savers lined up outside of banks to get their money back. This is called "a run on the bank." A run on the bank is caused primarily by the fractional-reserve system, a system that allows a bank to lend out more money than it holds in deposits.

If the government wanted to slow the economy, the U.S. Treasury and the Federal Reserve Bank would lower the fractional reserve to, let's say, 5. That means, for every dollar you and I put in, the bank can lend out $5. With fewer dollars to borrow, interest rates go up and the economy slows.

As you may have already noticed, the fractional-reserve system of banking destroys the purchasing power of your savings by magically printing money out of thin air every time you deposit your savings. This system is the same all over the world, a system mandated by the World Bank and the IMF, the International Monetary Fund.

With a fractional reserve of 10, a more complete diagram is as follows:

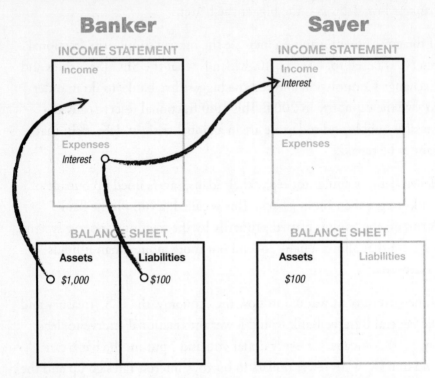

The real magic occurs when the banker pays the saver, let's say, 2 percent interest and lends out magic money through the fractional reserve at 5 percent to 25 percent.

Let's be conservative:

Saver: $100 x 2 percent = $2 a year

Borrowers: $1000 x 10 percent = $100 a year.

In this example, the bank earns $100 on the saver's deposit of $100 and pays the saver only $2 for the use of the saver's money. This is why bankers love borrowers.

Keeping It Simple

If this is too confusing, all you need to know is that bankers need borrowers, not savers. If you and I stop borrowing, the economy stops running because today, all money is debt. In other words, "Debt makes the world go round."

Taxes Reward Debtors

Now you know why the tax department rewards debtors with tax-free money and punishes savers by taxing interest on savings at the highest taxable rate as earned, or ordinary, income.

Learning to Be a Debtor

In 1973, I returned home from Vietnam. I had been away from Hawaii since 1965. I was fortunate to be assigned to Marine Corps Air Station at Kaneohe Bay, Hawaii, for my last year of service.

I had left Hawaii as a boy of 18 and returned home as a young man of 26. I had respectfully listened to adults all my life. I had gone to school after receiving a Congressional appointment to a federal military academy in New York, and graduated with a bachelor of science degree. I got a job upon graduation, sailing for Standard Oil as a third mate on their oil tankers, and earned a lot of money for a kid of 21 years of age. I was earning nearly twice as much as dad, who was nearly 50.

Rather than make a career of Standard Oil and one day become a ship's captain, I resigned. I joined the Marine Corps, earning $200 a month as a Marine lieutenant, which was a lot less than the $4,000 a month I was earning at Standard Oil. My flight training began at Pensacola, Florida, where it took two years to graduate and receive my wings.

In 1971, I was immediately transferred to Camp Pendleton, California, for advanced training and was stationed on board an aircraft carrier in Vietnam in 1972. I crashed three times that year and was glad to return home to Hawaii in 1973, still in one piece.

Now that I was home and about to leave the military, it was time to think for myself. I was 26 years old, and I knew it was time that I decided what I wanted to do when I grew up.

The new airbase was only 15 minutes from my poor dad's home and 30 minutes from my rich dad's office in Waikiki. During my final year as a pilot, I visited both men and sought their advice for my future.

My poor dad thought I should fly for the airlines, as most of my fellow pilots were doing. When I told him I was done flying, he suggested I go back to Standard Oil and sail as a third mate. He told me, "The pay is great, and you'll have five months off a year so you only have to work seven months a year." When I shook my head to that idea, he recommended that I return to school, get my master's degree, possibly my doctorate degree, and then get a job with the government. My response to that was, "I'd rather go back to fight in Vietnam."

I had a problem with my dad's advice about going back to school and working for the government. It was the same advice he had followed in his life, advice that did not work for him. At the age of 54, he was unemployed and living off his savings. His life's plan failed when he resigned as the head of education for the State of Hawaii to run for lieutenant governor as a Republican. The Democratic ticket had his boss running for reelection. When my dad lost, he was blacklisted from government service in Hawaii.

It disturbed me, listening to him advise me to do what did not work for him. He thought I should work for the government in the E quadrant. My dad's unemployment at the age of 54, highly educated and hardworking though he was, presented to me a glimpse of the future, the future we are in today.

I thanked my dad and drove to my rich dad's office in Waikiki. I now knew which dad's advice I wanted to follow. I knew that what I wanted when I grew up was to become an entrepreneur who operated out of the B and I quadrants.

Learn to Invest in Debt

In 1973, my rich dad said there were three things I needed to learn if I wanted to follow in his footsteps. They were:

1. **Learn to sell.** The ability to sell is the most important skill of an entrepreneur. The most important job of an entrepreneur is to raise money.
2. **Learn to invest via market trends.** Today, this is called technical analysis, predicting the future of markets by tracking the past.
3. **Learn to invest in real estate.** Learn how to manage debt to achieve wealth.

Rich dad was very aware of Nixon's change in the rules of money in 1971. That is why, in 1972 while I was in Vietnam, rich dad suggested I follow gold in the papers and take note of how the Vietnamese people responded to the changes in money. In *Conspiracy of the Rich,* I wrote about handing a Vietnamese fruit vendor a $50 bill and having her turn it down. She was my glimpse into the future and the coming crisis with the dollar, a crisis that is still coming.

When I asked my rich dad to explain why I should take classes in real estate investing, he replied, "The dollar is no longer money. The dollar is now debt. If you want to be rich, you need to learn to use debt to grow your wealth."

When I asked if he would teach me, he replied, "No. Invest in your education first." He did not want to waste his time with someone who knew nothing about real estate and debt. Encouraging me to learn, he said, "I will guide you after you have done your courses. I will be your mentor and your coach, but first you must seek your own education."

I left his office a little dejected. I had no idea where to find any real estate-investor education. I knew there were courses to become a real estate agent, but I knew real estate agents are not investors. I knew this because my rich dad often made jokes about stockbrokers and real estate brokers, saying, "The reason they're called brokers is because they're broker than you are." Explaining further, he said, "Most real estate brokers take courses to get their license to sell real estate, not invest in real estate. A real estate license allows them to sell houses and earn money in the S quadrant. Most real estate agents know little to nothing about real estate in the I quadrant." Leaving his office, I knew I needed to find real estate education for the I quadrant. I knew I did not want to be a real estate broker in the S quadrant.

Late one night, as I prepared for an early morning flight at the Marine Air Station, an infomercial came on TV, enticing viewers to sign up for a real estate-investment course. I dialed the number on the screen and signed up for a free preview to be held in a few days. At the free seminar, I heard exactly what I wanted to hear and paid $385 for a three-day course to be held in a few weeks. At the time, $385 was a fortune for a Marine Corps pilot whose flight pay was less than $900 gross a month. Like most people, I had a mortgage, car payment, and other expenses. My mind went crazy as I wondered if I was being smart or foolish. I wondered if I was being taken and if I would walk away with nothing.

That $385 turned out to be one of the best investments I have ever made. That course has made me multimillions of dollars, over and over again, much of it tax-free. More important than the money is the impact that course has had on our lives. Investing in our education, through that course, is one of the reasons Kim and I were able to become financially free, Kim at 37 and me at 47.

In 1973, I did exactly what the instructor of the real estate course taught us to do. I spent weeks looking at different investments. At every real estate office, the real estate agents told me the same thing, "You cannot find those deals in Hawaii. Hawaii is too expensive."

I was prepared for this closed-minded chatter from real estate agents because the course instructor had warned us, saying, "That is why they are real estate agents and not real estate investors. If they were investors, they would not need to be sales people."

After weeks of searching and hearing over and over, "You can't do that here. What you want does not exist," I finally found a tiny real estate office on a back street of Waikiki and found the answers I had been searching for. When I said to the broker, "I'm looking for an investment property in a great area, low priced, very little to zero down, and something that has positive cash flow," he smiled and said, "I have what you're looking for. In fact, I have nearly 35 of them."

Three days later, I flew to the island of Maui, rented a car and drove 45 minutes to the property. Once there, I could not believe my eyes. The project was spectacular. It was across the street from a beautiful, isolated sandy beach, just like in the post cards of old Hawaii. The reason the prices were so good is because the entire property was in foreclosure. Everything was for sale. Like a kid in a candy store, I went from unit to unit, looking for the one I wanted.

Finally, I chose one. The price for any unit was $18,000. The terms: 10 percent down, or $1800, with the seller financing the balance.

This meant I did not to have to qualify for a bank loan. It was everything all the other real estate brokers said did not exist, and it was on the island of Maui, near one of the most desirable resorts on the island.

Once I knew the property would generate cash flow, even with 100 percent financing, I pulled out my credit card, putting the $1,800 down payment on the card. I had none of my own money in the investment, and I still made money. Eventually, I bought a total of three of these properties. I would have bought more, but my credit card was at its limit.

Things went well for about six months. Then all hell broke loose. The septic system in the project broke, raw sewage rolled into my best unit, and I learned about negative cash flow and the dangers of being in too much debt. The moment the septic system broke and my tenant moved out, my asset turned into a liability. Rather than making $20 a month, I was losing $300 a month. I was facing the nightmare that keeps most investors out of real estate: property management and negative cash flow.

My real-life education had begun. Thank God my two other units were still operating. I was learning how to use debt to become rich and how debt can make you poor. It was the start of a priceless education in the power of debt.

Today, real estate brokers continue to say to Kim and me, "You can't do that." They say that, even though they see us buying 300- to 500-unit apartment complexes with debt and making millions tax-free. Most real estate agents can't do what we do because they were educated in the S quadrant, rather than the I quadrant.

Since debt can be lethal, we recommend you start small. Buy a number of small deals, as Kim did when she bought her first 20 units. Learn how to manage debt and manage real estate.

As most people know, getting into debt is easy. Managing debt is hard.

Why Are So Many People in Trouble?

FAQ

Why are so many people in trouble with debt?

Short Answer

They use debt to buy liabilities. The rich use debt to buy assets.

Explanation

In *Rich Dad Poor Dad,* I stated that your house is not an asset. The reason most homes are not assets is simply because the owner pays the mortgage, taxes, insurance, and upkeep. With our properties, the tenants pay for those expenses, plus our profit.

We use debt to finance assets, things that put money in our pockets. It doesn't have to be real estate. For example, Kim and I own a 58-foot sailboat. For most people, a boat is a big liability, a hole in the water you pour money into. Our boat is an asset because the boat is in a charter business, so tourists pay for the debt, insurance, upkeep, and boat slip rental. We make money every month and use the boat when we please.

Remember, it is not the asset class that determines if something (a house, boat, business, oil, or gold) is an asset or a liability. What determines if something is an asset is the direction of the cash flow. If cash flows into your pocket, it's an asset. If cash flows out of your pocket, it's a liability. It's that simple, in theory. In practice is where the challenge lies.

Real-Life Real Estate

FAQ

Would you give us a real-life example of how you achieve 100 percent debt and still have positive cash flow?

Short Answer

Sure.

Real-Life Example

I'm pulling this example from a project Kim and I have with our real estate partner, Ken McElroy. Ken and his partner, Ross McAllister, put the deal together, did the work, and manage the property. Kim and I are financial partners in the project.

Project: 144 apartment units + 10 acres vacant land

Location: Tucson, Arizona

Tucson is a city with strong job growth from the University of Arizona, the military, and government agencies such as the U.S. Border Patrol. Since many jobs are transient, there is a high demand for rental housing.

The property was not listed with real estate agents. Ken and Ross were the property managers of the property. When the owner said he wanted to sell, the project changed hands to Ken, Ross, Kim, me, and two other investors.

As you may know, most great deals are not listed. Most great deals go to insiders.

Price: $7.6 million ($7.1 million for the 144 units and $500,000 for the vacant land)

Financing: $2.6 million in equity from investors
$5 million via a new loan

Plan: Build 108 new units on the 10 acres.

Financing for addition: $5 million to build the 108 new units
The existing property and the 10 acres were used as collateral for the new $5 million construction loan.

Total units: 252 units when complete

Total package: $2.6 million equity + *$10 million debt*

New basis: $12.6 million

New appraisal: $18 million.

An increase in rents increased the appraisal.

New financing: 75 percent leverage = $13.5 million
($18 million x 75 percent = $13.5 million)

Paid off old loans: $13.5 million - $10.0 million = $3.5 million

Return to investors: $3.5 million

Net transaction: Kim and I invested $1 million.
From the $3.5 million return to investors, we received $1.4 million.
$1.4 million is reinvested in a 350-unit property in Oklahoma.

Taxes on $1.4 million: 0

Today, Kim, Ken, Ross, and I still own the 252 units in Tucson. We receive monthly income from the property. Since we have zero invested in the property, our ROI (return on investment) is infinite.

Over the course of seven years, Kim and I have invested in over 2,500 units with Ken and Ross, using the same investment strategy. Today's economic climate has offered us opportunities to buy even more properties because prices are low and, more importantly, interest rates are very low. Low interest rates increase our income as rental income goes up. Rental income is going up because fewer people can afford to buy their own home, so they rent.

During the real estate bubble between 2005 and 2007, Kim, Ken, Ross, and I were losing renters because they were using subprime financing to buy homes they could not afford. During that bubble, we actually made less money. But once the bubble burst, the tenants flowed back in, our cash flow increased, and our apartment properties increased in value as the values of residential homes plunged.

When banks look at large, multi-million-dollar projects, they focus on the borrower's track record and the property itself. They make their lending decision primarily on cash flow, not the borrower.

When homeowners buy their home, banks focus on the borrower and the homeowner's income because there is no income on a personal residence.

The good news is that the same strategy can apply to small real estate investments. I used 100 percent financing to buy my first apartments on Maui. While not all investments work that way, this is our objective: We want our down payment back, a free asset, free cash flow, and tax breaks. Kim, Ken, Ross, and I call an infinite return "printing money."

Infinite Return

FAQ
What is an infinite return?

Short Answer
Money for nothing.

Explanation
If I have zero in the asset and I receive $1, a return on zero is infinite. It is money for nothing. The asset is free, once we get our money back.

Keeping this overly simple, I'll use the following for an example. Let's say a property costs $100,000 and my down payment is $20,000. If I receive $200 net positive cash-flow income after all expenses (including mortgage payment), I have a 1 percent monthly return on my investment of $20,000. That's a 12 percent annual return or $2,400 per year.

ROI is net income, divided by down payment.

$200	1 percent per month, or
$20,000	12 percent per year

Our investment strategy is to get that $20,000 back and continue to receive $200 a month. Once the $20,000 is returned, the ROI is infinite.

This is the investment scenario I was looking for when I finished the real estate course in 1973. This is what most real estate agents said was impossible. Today, we continue to strive for the impossible.

To most people, $200 a month, a 1 percent monthly return, looks sickly, certainly not exciting. Yet if you own 100 of these small deals, that is $20,000 a month in cash flow. And 1,000 properties is $200,000 a month. That is more money than most doctors and lawyers make in a month.

When Kim started out, her goal was 20 units. She accomplished that in 18 months because the economy was terrible. It's not that different today.

Once she had her 20 properties, she sold them tax-deferred. With her tax-deferred capital gains, she purchased two larger apartment houses, one 29 units and one 18 units. Today, following the infinite-return formula, she has nearly 3,000 apartment units, commercial buildings, a luxury resort and five golf courses—all with positive cash flow, even in down markets. Her goal is to add at least 500 more units every year, using the same formula—the formula most real estate agents say does not exist. This difference in mind-set underscores the difference between real estate education in the S quadrant and the I quadrant. The real irony is that real estate agents pay taxes on the income they earn, and investors receive massive tax breaks on their income.

On most of our investments, we have no money of our own in the property. If we do have money in the property, we are always in the process of getting that money back. In most cases, it takes a year to five years for our money to return.

Once we get our money back, we move it to acquire more assets. This is a formula known as "the velocity of money." I wrote about the velocity of money in greater detail in *Rich Dad's Who Took My Money? Why Slow Investors Lose and Fast Money Wins!*, published in 2004. Our formula has not changed, and it has picked up velocity in this horrible economy. If you had taken the action suggested in *Who Took My Money?* before the crash, you might be getting your money back today.

Ken McElroy Shares How to Use Debt

Have you ever wondered why your checking account is free? Banks need your deposits so they can lend money. Banks can't make money until they have your money to lend. At this point, you have two choices: Use bank debt to make you rich, or use bank debt to make others rich.

Great wealth is founded on the use of debt. There is good debt, and there is bad debt.

If you borrow money and spend it on something that goes up in value, that's good debt. If you borrow money and spend it on something that will go down in value, that's bad debt. You use good debt to enhance your situation and increase your net worth. You should avoid bad debt altogether.

Debt is leverage. Everything you use it for will be magnified, good or bad. If you borrow money for a liability like a car that will eventually be worthless, you are magnifying your cost negatively. Bad debt creates a liability that takes money out of your pocket.

Using debt as leverage can also be an extremely positive experience when you are buying assets.

My business uses debt and leverage to create wealth for my investors by purchasing assets, specifically multi-family property. These properties not only produce a monthly cash flow, but they grow in value over time using sound management principles.

A good example of using good debt and leverage is when a group of investors, including Robert and Kim Kiyosaki, bought a 288-unit property located in Broken Arrow, Oklahoma, a suburb of Tulsa. This property was well located, and we had several opportunities to increase the revenue and decrease the expenses.

At purchase, the property appraised for over $14 million. Value is always based on the net cash flow. Using the appraisal, the bank allowed us to assume the first mortgage of $9,750,000 at 4.99 percent interest rate. We also applied and were approved for a second mortgage of $1,090,000 at a 6.5 percent interest rate. This is an example of good debt.

The bank gave us these loans because the property had a high occupancy rate, and they knew the rents we would collect from the residents would more than pay the monthly mortgage payments.

We raised $3.4 million from investors for the down payment and for capital needs.

All along, our strategy was to install new washers and dryers in all the units, which could eventually get us an additional $25 in rent per unit, a total of $86,400 in additional income annually. (Math: 288 units x $25 x 12 months = $86,400).

In just three and a half years, we have been able to increase this property's annual net operating income by over $300,000. The original mortgage has decreased more than $600,000 because we paid the mortgage using the residents' rental payments during that same period of time.

Today, this property is now worth about $20 million. The value is increased because the net cash flow increased.

By using good debt and leverage and with just $3.4 million down, this property's value has increased by over $6 million, nearly $2 million a year. The annual cash flow also increased by over $300,000 and is distributed to the investors.

The original business plan was always to refinance using new debt and to leverage and return the original investor equity. In late 2011, we plan on refinancing this property with new debt and leverage with a new $15 million low-interest fixed-rate loan, which will pay off the existing $10 million in loans and leave $5 million to distribute.

There is nothing better than returning investors' money. In this case, if the proceeds are $5 million, we will return not only the original $3.4 million but an additional $1.6 million. Don't forget the investors also receive a nice monthly cash flow while the money is invested!

Once the investors receive their money back in full, their investment in this property will be zero. The "returned original investment" and additional proceeds are tax-free because it is a refinance.

In 2012 with a new loan in place, the property will continue to pay out cash flow to all the investors, which will create an infinite return.

I do want to emphasize that this scenario was planned from the beginning. Investors using leverage and debt are able to reap the rewards of the increased value on the "loaned" amount.

If you use good debt and buy assets that generate cash flow, you can become very wealthy.

Tom Wheelwright on Love from the Government

The tax law is a series of stimulus packages for business owners and investors. Nowhere is this more true than for real estate investors. I'm not talking about people who fix and flip real estate. They are not investors. I'm talking about those who buy, improve, and hold on to real estate for long-term investment.

As an incentive for investors to buy, improve, and hold real estate, the government gives two primary tax benefits. The first and largest is depreciation. Depreciation is a deduction you receive over time for the cost of the property, whether you bought it with your money or with someone else's money (debt). Here is how it works.

Suppose you purchase a rental property for $200,000, using $20,000 or 10 percent of your own money and $180,000 or 90 percent of the bank's money. What did you really buy? You bought land worth, say, $40,000 and improvements, including a building, landscaping and fixtures, of $160,000.

The government lets you take a deduction, called depreciation, for the wear and tear on the building. If this is a residential property, your deduction is about 3.64 percent per year in the United States. (It's more in some other countries.)

That means that you get a deduction on your tax return of almost $6,000 per year for depreciation ($160,000 x 3.64 percent). Let's say your cash flow is 1 percent per month on your initial investment of $20,000. That means you will have cash flow of $2,400 per year. With a tax deduction of $6,000, you will show a loss on your tax return of $3,600 per year ($2,400 minus $6,000). This $3,600 loss can be used to reduce your taxes from your salary, your business or your other investments. So depreciation protects your cash flow from taxes and produces an additional tax benefit by lowering your taxes from your other income. And remember that you get depreciation, not only on the dollars you invest, but also on the money the bank loaned.

You get a similar benefit called amortization, which refers to your costs of borrowing money from the bank, such as points and loan-origination fees. You get to take the deduction for amortization even if the bank loaned you the money to pay the fees.

These tax benefits are yours even though the property may be appreciating, or going up in value. So real estate gives you benefits through depreciation, amortization, and through appreciation in value.

There are additional tax benefits as well for real estate investors. When you sell your real estate, you have a choice on what you pay in taxes. If you decide to cash out, you can pay tax at the low capital-gains rate on any appreciation in your property. If you decide instead to use the proceeds from your sale to invest in another property, you can pay no tax. This is called a "like-kind" or 1031 exchange.

What's more, if you sell your property at a loss, you get to take the loss as an ordinary loss. This means that you can use the loss to offset any other type of income. This is quite different than if you were selling a stock or mutual fund, where a loss would be limited to offsetting gains from other capital assets. So if your property appreciates, you pay little or no tax, and if your property loses value, you get to use the losses to offset your ordinary income. Many countries have similar rules and tax rates on the sale of real estate and other business assets.

Can you begin to see how the tax laws provide stimulus to real estate investors and business owners? (By the way, in the United States, flippers get none of these benefits and in fact, have to pay an additional tax, called self-employment tax, that investors don't have to pay.) The tax laws are directions from your government on how they want you to use your money to improve the economy. This is especially true when you are using debt to invest in real estate and business.

I'll let Robert share some more ideas about using debt to invest.

Different ROI

Most stockbrokers or real estate agents talk about a 10 percent return as being a good return. But in most cases, that is a 10 percent return on capital gains, not cash flow. It's not real money. Again, that is the problem with getting your financial education in the S quadrant. (In most cases, S can stand for sales.) As an investor, I must know what kind of ROI the sales person is talking about. Is it 10 percent on cash flow or capital gains, and what are the tax consequences? Am I punished with taxes, or given tax breaks? More importantly, how do I achieve an infinite return (aka "money for nothing" or "printing my own money")?

If you know what you are doing, debt can be an unfair advantage.

The Secret of the I Quadrant

The secret of the I quadrant is OPM: other people's money. As you know, many people invest, but they use their own money.

To be a true I, a person needs to learn how to use OPM to invest, either from banks, pension funds, or private investors.

A smart investor can use OPM in any asset class, including stocks, precious metals such as gold, and commodities such as oil. OPM is the secret of the I quadrant, regardless of asset class. Once you learn the secret, you will see it used everywhere.

When Kim invested in her first house, she put down $5,000 and borrowed $40,000. The moment she did that, she became a true investor, using OPM to invest. When I used my credit card to buy the $18,000 units on Maui, I was using 100 percent debt to finance my investments. The moment I did this, I moved into the I quadrant.

When Kim and I invested $1 million with Ken and Ross, we did so because their business plan was to use bank money to get our money back. If they said we had to leave the $1 million in forever, we would not have invested. We got our $1 million back in three and a half years. We use OPM as much as possible because we want our money back, plus we want to keep the asset, plus we want the cash flow, *and* we want tax advantages. That is what true I-quadrant investors do.

When I invest in oil, I use OPM from the government and from the oil companies to buy my oil wells for me. When I invest in stocks, I use options and market momentum to buy my assets for me.

My rich dad often said, "Only lazy and foolish people use their own money." OPM is the secret of real investors.

Final Questions

FAQ

Won't the government plug this loophole?

Short Answer

Anything is possible, but I doubt it.

Explanation

I stated earlier that after 1971, money became debt. For the economy to grow, the economy needs debtors. This is why the government's taxes punish savers and incentivize debtors, especially debtors who can take on large amounts of debt.

If the government took away this debt loophole, the economy would seize up immediately, chaos would break out, and the crowd would roast the politicians. If the government does close this loophole, they will open others for their friends, friends with money who finance their campaigns.

FAQ

Isn't it cruel for people who do not know how to use debt?

Short Answer

Very cruel. I laugh and I cry every time I see someone win the lottery or a young sports athlete receive a $50 million contract to play professional sports. What is the first thing these people do? They rush out to buy a big house and nice cars, not only for themselves, but also for their family and friends. Rather than use their money to get richer, they use their money to fall deeply into debt, debt for liabilities. It is not long before their money is transferred back to the government and the rich. In the end, the foolish person is only left with debt.

FAQ

What happens if the federal government starts printing money and hyper-inflation sets in?

Short Answer

That would be wonderful. I would pay off my loans with cheaper dollars and raise my rents to keep up with inflation.

FAQ

What if you're wrong and the economy collapses and your renters cannot pay the rent?

Short Answer

No problem.

Explanation

Most of our loans are *non-recourse* loans. If we cannot pay the loans, we give the property back to the bank. Non-recourse means the bank cannot go after any other assets we own.

My rich dad often said, "If you owe the bank $20,000 and cannot pay your loan, *you have a problem.* If you owe the bank $20,000,000 and you cannot pay your loan, *the bank has a problem.*"

Today, banks are very careful when lending millions of dollars. That is why you should take real estate investment classes and learn to become an investor, not a real estate agent. Real estate investors must know how to manage debt and their properties.

No matter how much money you have, start small. Invest in many small deals, practicing to gain experience in managing debt, property, and tenants. Once a banker knows you have experience and a successful track record, they will lend you as much as you can handle.

Final Word

Every day, billions of dollars are being printed. Every day, there are trillions of dollars looking for a home. The reason there is a growing number of poor educated people is because they have never been taught how to access this multi-trillion-dollar pool of money. Most people are standing next to this massive ocean of money, afraid to jump in because they never learned how to swim.

In 1997, *Rich Dad Poor Dad* stated: "Your house is not an asset." Hate mail poured in from realtors from all over the world.

In 2006 in Phoenix, a rather obnoxious real estate agent ran television commercials encouraging people to buy real estate because prices were going up. Four years later, that same real estate agent ran television commercials encouraging the people who had bought houses from him to let him get rid of their houses that had now gone down in value.

Again, that is the difference between real estate education in the S quadrant and real estate education in the I quadrant.

The really sad thing is that in 2010, interest rates were really low and banks were giving away great real estate. It was a time for the rich to get richer, while, ironically, the poor were getting poorer.

As the Bible states: "My people perish from a lack of knowledge." Today, millions of people are perishing because they do not know the difference between assets and liabilities. Millions are perishing because they work hard for money while governments are printing trillions of dollars, which means an increase in taxes and inflation. Then these same people try to save money and use bad debt to acquire liabilities, liabilities they think are assets. This is financial insanity.

The unfair advantage is the knowledge to use debt to acquire assets, assets that produce cash flow for an infinite return—and to know not to save money, because money is no longer money. Money is now debt, and that is why savers are losers.

UNFAIR ADVANTAGE #4:
RISK

FAQ

Is real estate a good investment?

Answer

I don't know. Are you a good real estate investor?

FAQ

Are stocks a good investment?

Answer

I don't know. Are you a good stock investor?

FAQ

Is a business a good investment?

Answer

I don't know. Are you a good entrepreneur?

You get my point. Without financial education, you will lose your money, regardless of what you invest in.

Extreme Risk

On a regular basis I hear, "I just hate risk. I'd rather play it safe. I have enough challenges." In their avoidance of risk, people lead lives of extreme risk.

Oxymoron

The definition of oxymoron is: "Words that contradict each other." Examples are: jumbo shrimp, government service, painless dentist, honest politician and holy war.

In the world of money, the following are also oxymorons:

1. Job Security
2. Saving Money
3. Safe Investments
4. Fair Share
5. Mutual Fund
6. Diversified Portfolio
7. Debt-Free

People who seek to avoid risk the most use these oxymorons the most. These oxymorons guide them into a life of extreme risk.

Those with financial education know why these words are financial oxymorons. To those without financial education, these oxymorons sound like financial words of wisdom. I will explain:

1. **Job Security**

   When I graduated from high school, many of my classmates did not go on to college. They did not have to because there were many high-paying jobs waiting for high school graduates. Many of the thousands of jobs on the pineapple and sugar plantations were high-paying jobs for heavy equipment operators, cannery workers, and clerical workers. Most were unionized jobs with good pay and great benefits.

   Today, most of those plantations are gone. My classmates either work for McDonald's or became entrepreneurs in "tropical agriculture," aka marijuana. Many are doing just fine as outlaw farmers. Obviously, they do not pay much in taxes. To the outside world, they look like poor people collecting welfare, yet they drive late-model pickup trucks paid for in cash.

Ironically, due to the current economic crisis and technology, many of my classmates who went on to college are the ones in financial trouble. One of the smartest and prettiest girls in my school, a few years younger than I am, a graduate of an elite small college in New England, is now unemployed and lives in the woods of rural Hawaii, almost a hermit. She is waiting to be old enough to collect Social Security and Medicare.

Once President Nixon opened trade with China, jobs flowed overseas as our dollars helped China build new factories. As China built massive factories for low-wage workers, high-priced laborers in the United States were no longer needed. Middle-management positions for college graduates also began to disappear.

Not only are low-wage jobs flowing overseas, but technology is also eliminating high-paying jobs. Technology is a growing reason for job security to be an oxymoron. In the 1920s, over 2 million Americans worked for the railroads. Today, railroads operate efficiently with fewer than 300,000 workers. Fewer workers mean increased profits for the owners of the railroads, owners like Warren Buffett, who in 2009 paid $34 billion to buy Burlington Northern Santa Fe railroad. Advances in technology eliminated jobs, and the reduced labor costs translated to profits for the owners. Why did Buffett buy a railroad rather than a hot new technology company? The answer is simple: steady cash flow.

Jobs will continue to be lost because American workers are paid 40 times more than the lowest-wage workers in the world. This means jobs are not coming back. Even China, once a low-wage country, is in trouble as Chinese workers want higher wages. As Chinese workers earn more, jobs migrate to even lower-wage countries such as the Philippines, North Korea, Kyrgyzstan, and Indonesia.

With breakthroughs in technology, it is the owners of businesses who win and the employees who lose. Even in Silicon Valley, where much of the new technology is created, manufacturing takes place outside of America. The computer I use to write this book was designed in the United States and manufactured in China. As I am writing this book, I know that in a few months it will be on sale in several different languages in e-book and hard-copy format. After this book is written, my costs drop as income comes in from the asset I created.

My business is expanding worldwide with fewer employees than in years past. Technology is a growing unfair advantage for those in the B quadrant and sometimes a disadvantage for those in the E and S quadrants.

Those with job security will pay more and more in taxes. With growing national debt, governments will be raising taxes. The quadrants with the least wiggle room in minimizing taxes are employees in the E quadrant and specialists like doctors and lawyers in the S quadrant. In 2010, the government increased tax breaks for those in B and I quadrants but increased taxes on those in the E and S quadrants.

Rising unemployment is not just a problem in the United States. It is a problem worldwide, even in China. Prolonged unemployment leads to social unrest, political revolution, and then overthrow of the government. This is why most countries will do almost anything to steal jobs from other countries.

Playing Games with Money
To keep jobs and people employed, countries are playing games with their money. By keeping their money weak, through exchange rates or just printing a lot of it, a country's exports are cheaper. If a country's currency strengthens and becomes more expensive, their exports become expensive, exports fall, and jobs are lost.

In 1966 when I first traveled to Japan as a student on board a U.S. cargo ship, the U.S. dollar could buy 360 yen. As a student, I could buy a lot with my dollar. Japan was cheap for an American.

Today, the U.S. dollar buys approximately 90 yen. This means the yen got stronger and the dollar weaker. Today, Japan is expensive for Americans.

If Japan wants to save their economy, they need to weaken the yen, maybe moving it back up to 150 yen to a dollar. American exports will then become expensive, we will export less, and thus lose jobs.

Keeping people employed is one reason that countries play games with their money.

The War of Money

Today, the United States and China are in a 'war of money.' The United States wants China to raise the value of their money so we can export more to them and import less. China knows that if the value of their money increases so does China's unemployment.

In retaliation, the United States keeps devaluing the dollar and China devalues their currency, the yuan. Weaker currency means inflation at home.

This is one reason that the next oxymoron, save money, is ridiculous. Why save money when countries are weakening their money, making money less valuable and shopping at Walmart more expensive?

We have to weaken the dollar if we want to save jobs. Because with a weak dollar, we can export more. This means there will be more demand for manufactured American goods, which means there will be more jobs.

The foregoing are a few reasons why *job security* is an oxymoron.

Fin Ed History

The worst dictators in modern history came to power during times of financial crisis. Hitler came to power in Germany, Mao came to power in China, Lenin in Russia, and Milosevic in Serbia and Yugoslavia during an economic crisis.

Hitler and U.S. President Franklin Delano Roosevelt (FDR) came to power in the same year, 1933. FDR, while greatly loved, created many of the financial institutions that caused many of the financial challenges the United States faces today. Some of his creations are Social Security, Federal Deposit Insurance Corporation (FDIC), and the Federal Housing Administration (FHA). He also took the United States off the gold standard in 1933.

Many people believe it was World War II that brought us out of the Depression. While the war did increase U.S. productivity and its balance of payments, it was the Bretton Woods Agreement of 1944 that restored the gold standard and increased the power of the U.S. dollar and the United States in the world. In 1971, Nixon broke the Bretton Woods Agreement with the world and today we are in a crisis again, facing a possible new depression.

The collapse of the gold agreement is known as the "Nixon shock." After 1971, prosperity was created in America through debt and inflation rather than manufacturing goods that the world wanted to buy.

Without the discipline of gold, the Federal Reserve Bank embarked upon a process known as systematic inflation. The United States enjoyed good years because the economy was based upon ever-larger quantities of counterfeit money. America's national debt is a Ponzi scheme of debt and fiat currency, paying off debt with taxpayer dollars that are worth less and less.

This system survives as long as the rest of the world goes along with the cash heist. If the world wakes up to the fantasy that you can buy things with phony money, the fantasy is over. If the U.S. dollar goes, the United States will go with it.

This is where we are, as I write in 2011: Americans are in debt for generations to come.

2. Saving Money

Why save money when our governments are weakening the purchasing power of our money?

As you know, after 1971, money stopped being money and became debt.

Prior to 1971, the United States was required to have gold backing the dollar. But when the United States was importing more than we were exporting, gold was flowing out of the United States. When France demanded payment in gold, Nixon took the dollar off the gold standard.

After 1971, if the United States needed money, they just printed money. Today, they do not need a printing press. Today money is digital, just an electronic blip on a screen.

To create money, the U.S. Treasury issues a T-bond, T-bill, or T-note, which is simply an IOU from the taxpayers of the United States.

Let's say the U.S. Treasury issues a $10 million T-bill.

Private investors, banks, and countries such as China, Japan, and England buy this T-bill, which is debt, an IOU. Many people like U.S. debt because our debt is considered the safest of all debt, especially since we can print money to pay off our debt.

The problem is that if the world suddenly does not want our debt, the Fed will print even more counterfeit money. This will lead to inflation and possibly hyperinflation.

Quantitative Easing

If no one shows up to buy U.S. Treasury debt, then the Federal Reserve Bank steps in, writes a check (even if there is nothing in its account) and buys the bond. When the Fed writes a check, it is creating money out of thin air, which is the reason they call it *quantitative easing*. The reason they changed the name from *printing money* to *quantitative easing* is because it sounds more intelligent, even though it is financial suicide.

If you or I wrote a check without money in the bank account, we would go to jail.

This is why *saving money* is an oxymoron.

Fin Ed Definitions

T-bills, T-notes, and T-bonds are debt issued by the U.S. Treasury. The difference between the three is the length of maturity.

- T-bills are issued for terms less than a year.
- T-notes are issued for terms of 2, 3, 5, and 10 years.
- T-bonds are issued for terms of 10 years or more.

Fin Ed Definitions

Inflation vs. hyperinflation: **Inflation simply means there is more money chasing fewer goods and services.**

Hyperinflation has little to do with money supply, as many people believe. Hyperinflation can be an excess of money or a shortage of money. The issue with hyperinflation is simply that no one wants the money, regardless of how much or how little there is. In hyperinflation, money is as valuable as used toilet paper. No one wants it. It becomes a joke.

To pay for the Revolutionary War, the Continental Congress created the Continental Dollar. The problem was that the war lasted a long time and they kept printing Continentals to pay soldiers and buy war supplies. When the Continental's value went to zero, soldiers and suppliers were left with nothing, hence the saying, "Not worth a Continental."

When the Civil War broke out, the Confederate States printed the Confederate Dollar with the same results.

Germany did the same thing after World War I, and the German people began using the Reichsmark for wallpaper, to start fires, and probably for toilet paper. When the German economy collapsed, Adolf Hitler came to power in 1933, the same year President Franklin Delano Roosevelt took the dollar off the gold standard.

In my wallet I carry a fresh Zimbabwe $100 trillion note, which numerically is $100,000,000,000,000. At one time, it bought three eggs. It purchases less today.

Today, Federal Reserve Bank Chairman Ben Bernanke is printing trillions of dollars and President Obama is spending trillions of dollars.

Phony money causes wars between nations as well as wars of real money (gold, silver, food, oil, things with intrinsic value) versus pieces of paper with ink on it.

3. **Safe Investments**

    There is no such thing as a safe investment. There are only smart investors.

    As stated at the start of this chapter, when I am asked questions such as, "Is real estate a good investment?" or "Are stocks good investments?" my answer is always the same, "Are you a good investor?"

    No investment is safe if you are foolish, even gold. You can lose a lot of money investing in real money, gold and silver.

    Today, in 2011, gold is hitting all-time highs because fools rush in to chase fool's gold. Gold fever is creating fools rushing in as gold prices rise, just as they did when stocks and real estate went in bubbles. As I write, gold is over $1,300 an ounce, an all-time high, but not if measured in 1980 dollars when gold hit $850 an ounce and silver hit $50 an ounce. For gold to be at an all-time high, it would need to be at $2,400 in today's dollars.

    Today, I see the frenzy in gold. Everywhere I go, I see signs, "We buy gold." You know the buyer will pay $300 an ounce, not $1300 an ounce to the seller, desperate for cash and selling his or her mother's jewelry.

Even when a person invests in gold coins, many new investors are fooled by fool's gold, buying "rare gold coins," aka numismatic coins. A friend of a friend was all excited about buying a rare gold coin from the last depression. He paid nearly $3,000 for a coin that was worth $1,200.

I believe it is possible for gold to hit $3,000 an ounce in a few years, and I don't think $7,000 is out of the question. Does this mean you should go out and buy it? My answer is no. You still need to be educated on the gold markets, especially at these prices.

In overly simple terms and in theory, the price of gold is equal to the money supply. The more governments print money and increase the money supply, the more the price of gold goes up. Gold goes up as the purchasing power of the dollar goes down. This is why I think it's funny that Fed Chairman Bernanke stated on June 9, 2010: "I don't fully understand movements in the gold price."

This is the guy who is printing the money. He graduated from MIT, taught at Stanford and Harvard, is the expert on the last depression, now heads the most powerful bank in the world, and he does not understand the movements in the price of gold?

This is disturbing, but his lack of understanding makes him the best friend of gold investors. The more confused Chairman Bernanke is, the more I buy gold, silver, and oil.

Fed Chairman Bernanke reminds me of my poor dad, a college professor, a PhD, gazing out at the world from the mind-set of the E quadrant. If Bernanke worked out of the I quadrant, he might understand why the price of gold goes up with every dollar he prints, aka quantitative easing.

It is because of Federal Reserve Bank leaders like former Chairman

Greenspan and current Chairman Bernanke that I bought a gold mine in 1997. I knew they were destroying the dollar.

Kim and I also bought as much gold as possible before the year 2000, when gold was below $300 and silver was less than $3 an ounce.

For those considering saving precious metals rather than saving money, I would start with silver. In 2011, silver is a much better investment than gold. I say this because there is now more gold on planet earth than silver. Gold is also hoarded, which is why there is so much gold. Silver is used, much like oil, which is why there is much less silver than gold.

It is possible, someday in the not-too-distant future, that silver will be more expensive than gold. But please do not take my word for it. Do your own research.

For years, central banks were dumping gold and buying dollars. Today, they are dumping dollars and buying gold, increasing the price of gold, causing their currency to become worthless, and making life harder on the people of their country. Talk about the best-educated people doing stupid things.

My point is that you can lose money buying gold. If you had purchased gold in 1980, you would still be losing money today, even with gold at $1,300. The price of gold will need to hit $2,400 for you to have made your $850 in 1980 dollars back. If you can lose money buying gold, you can lose money buying anything.

This is why *safe investments* is an oxymoron.

4. **Fair Share**
Nothing is fair when it comes to money. God is not fair. If God were fair, I would look like Johnny Depp.

Nothing is fair in the stock market. Some people get more than their fair share for their shares. The average investor invests in the stock market buying shares of stock. But few investors know that there are different types of shares, and they are not fair. For example, there are *common* shares for the common man. The smart investors prefer to have *preferred* shares. Simply put, investors who own preferred shares receive preferential treatment over commoners who own common shares. Most mutual funds are filled with common shares.

There is another class of shares far above preferred shares. This level can be seen on the *CASHFLOW 101* game board.

Most of those in the Rat Race invest in preferred and common shares.

Investors at this level do not invest in shares. They invest in percentages.

When you perform your research of a public company by looking at a prospectus of a public company, you will see a category known as "selling shareholders." These are the shareholders who own large blocks of the stock, say 1 million to 10 million shares.

They are called "selling shareholders" because they sold only a *percentage* of their company and received a large block of shares. Building a business and taking your company public via an IPO (initial public offering) is another form of printing money, in this case, printing shares, or stock certificates.

When I took my gold mine public, Kim and I were selling shareholders, not buying shareholders.

There are differences between selling shareholders, preferred shareholders, and common shareholders.

This is why *fair share* is an oxymoron.

The Rich Dad Company is currently working on a book written by my mentor, the man who taught me how to build businesses and sell businesses via an IPO. If you want to learn how to become a selling shareholder, watch for this book.

Stay connected to Rich Dad – via Richdad.com – for the latest updates on books and our educational program for entrepreneurs.

5. **Mutual Fund**

There is nothing mutual about a mutual fund. A better term would be *one-sided* fund.

This does not mean I do not like mutual funds. Personally, I love mutual funds because mutual funds provide me the money to invest.

When I took my gold mine public via the IPO, it was a group of mutual-fund companies who purchased most of the stocks we offered.

Mutual funds are designed for people who know nothing about investing and feel more comfortable having a fund manager pick their common stocks for them.

The problem is that the investor puts up 100 percent of the money, takes 100 percent of the risk and receives only 20 percent of the profits (if there are profits). The mutual-fund company takes 80 percent of the investor's money via management fees and expenses. To me, this is a one-sided fund, not a mutual fund.

Making matters worse, taxes are not good on mutual funds.

Tom Wheelwright explains:

When you buy mutual funds, you are taxed in two separate ways. First, you are taxed on the capital gains when the fund trades (buys and sells) a stock. Second, you are taxed when you trade the mutual fund itself. The outcome of this taxing scheme is that you can pay capital gains on the mutual fund's stock trades in a year when the mutual fund goes down in value. Imagine paying taxes when you lose money. That's exactly what happens to a lot of people when they own mutual funds.

There are some advantages to mutual funds. Rather than have me discuss the pros and cons of mutual funds, I will let the Rich Dad advisor, Andy Tanner, explain paper assets.

Andy Tanner explains pros and cons of mutual funds:

When it comes to the pros and cons of mutual funds, I'd say that most of the pros lie in favor of the institutions that sell the mutual funds, along with the fund managers who collect fees from the fund's investors. The investors put up the money, investors assume the risk, and institutions and fund managers get paid whether the fund performs well or whether it doesn't. Combine that with a program of consistent dollar-cost averaging, and you have a constant flow of dollars coming into the fund at all times. As Robert says, there are always two sides to every coin, and there's no question that the mutual-fund companies are on the more profitable side.

I suppose the appeal of mutual funds, unit trusts, and retirement plans like 401(k)s and RRSPs is that, on the surface, they appear to give an investor a way to invest without having to have a lot of financial education. In addition, they also give the investor a sense of safety because they usually diversify the money across several different sectors.

The problem is simply that appearances can be deceiving. I'm not convinced at all that investing in a 401(k) filled with mutual funds is an alternative to financial education. The type of diversification that mutual funds carry gives rise to what I think is a very dangerous false sense of safety. In reality, they give an investor no more control than investing in a single stock. Risk is related to control. Less control means more risk, which is why hope is not a strategy.

I'd say there are at least four important problems with the predominant mutual fund/401(k) system that warrant an in-depth discussion with your financial advisor:

First, this brand of diversification does very little, if anything, to protect an investor against a large stock-market crash, a long-term stagnant stock market, or even a rising stock market that fails to outpace inflation over long periods.

When a person buys large amounts of stock in a single company (like Warren Buffett who bought millions of shares of Coca-Cola), a large concern is that the share price of the company can fall, which of course is beyond the control of the investor. By the same token, when a person is diversified across the market, it is still possible (if not likely) that the entire market will fall, which also is completely beyond the control of the investor. I think most people would agree that our world markets have become more volatile and probably more fragile than ever.

From the year 2000 to 2010 we've observed the "decade of nothing." Getting back to zero offers little consolation when growth—the exponential growth associated with compounding—was required to make a plan work and now retirement is staring the investor in the face. Moreover, we could easily have another decade of nothing or, even worse, a huge market slide (and there's plenty of fundamental data to suggest the latter). If you want to add to your financial vocabulary, the next time you're with your financial advisor, ask him to explain what "systemic risk" means. Most mutual funds and retirement plans make the dangerous assumption that the market will always go up in the long term, but there's no guarantee that that will actually happen for this generation of investors.

Second is the question of consistency. Standard & Poor's has released data that show that if a person takes a handful of mutual funds that do perform well in a given year, they almost never are able to repeat that performance over periods of five to ten years. In other words, past performance really is not a solid indication of future results.

Third is the question of fees. While most fees that go to the financial system can be found somewhere in the fine print, most of the investors I talk to have no idea what those fees are and how they will affect the outcome of their investments. In my soon-to-be-released Rich Dad's Advisor book *The ABCs of Investing in Stocks*, I dedicate nearly an entire chapter to helping investors understand the crippling ramifications that these fees bring to a person's 401(k) plan. When those who most vigorously defend the status quo of 401(k)s filled with mutual funds bray their message, consider how much money they are making with the status quo.

Fourth is the question of beating the market. Today it's not too hard to find financial instruments that are readily available to the individual investor that will at least mimic the market. Products like exchange-traded funds allow an investor to do pretty much everything that most mutual funds can do in terms of tracking an index market. Why should I pay huge expense ratios for a portfolio that is simply going to do whatever the market does anyway? If my 401(k) or 403(b) plan or IRA is simply going to mimic the market, what value does professional management bring? If a person examines their own IRA or 401(k), chances are they have done well when the market has done well, and they have hemorrhaged when the market has hemorrhaged. Sadly, most people find they're talented enough all by themselves to lose money when the market falls.

There's much more to the discussion than just these pros and cons. For many, the decisions they make will have a great impact on their financial future. In my opinion, this warrants a frank discussion with an advisor and serious consideration of a plan for financial education.

As Andy explained, mutual funds, banks, and pension companies are important because they provide the money that those in the B and I quadrants use to invest.

For the uneducated investor, *mutual funds* are an oxymoron, because they are one-sided funds, and are not mutually beneficial.

6. Diversified Portfolio

Most people are not diversified—they are *de-worsified*.

The four basic asset classes in the world of investments are shown in the asset column of the financial statement below.

Most people who believe they have a diversified portfolio are not diversified because they are primarily in only one asset class: paper assets.

Paper assets are made up of stocks, bonds, mutual funds, ETFs, insurance, annuities, and savings.

Again, they are not diversified, they are de-worsified. Even more hideous, mutual funds by definition are diversified, made up of a basket of different stocks, bonds, and paper assets. When a person has a diversified portfolio of mutual funds, he or she is beyond diversified.

When the stock market crashes as it did in 2007, most of the paper assets crash in unison. This is why even Warren Buffett's mutual fund, Berkshire Hathaway crashed in the crash.

As Buffett himself says, *"Diversification is protection against ignorance. (It) makes very little sense for those who know what they're doing."*

Jim Cramer, a very smart investor and an expert on the stock market, often runs a segment on his TV program called "Am I diversified?" During that segment, viewers call in and rattle off the stocks they are holding in their portfolios. For example, a viewer may say, "I have shares of Exxon, GE, IBM, Procter and Gamble, and Bank of America. I also have an emerging market fund, money market fund, a gold ETF, a bond fund, a REIT, an S&P 500 index fund, and I just bought an index fund for large cap dividends. Am I diversified?"

Jim Cramer then evaluates the viewer's diversified portfolio.

In my opinion, the above portfolio is not diversified. It is de worsified. It is *less worse,* but not diversified, because it is filled with only one class of assets: paper assets. If the stock market crashes, which it will, diversification will not protect him.

If the crash is severe, as it was in 1929 and 2007, the stock market may not recover for years, again destroying the portfolios for capital-gains investors.

Today, there are more mutual-fund companies than there are publicly traded companies. This is how insane diversification has become.

In 2007 when markets began to crash, everything crashed, even real estate. Diversification did not save millions of people from their lack of financial education.

For most people, their *diversified portfolio* is an oxymoron. It is a de-worsified portfolio, a portfolio made less worse, but not less risky.

Why Are Investors Losing?

FAQ
Why are uneducated investors losing so much?

Short Answer
They invest without insurance.

Explanation
You do not drive a car without insurance. You do not buy a house without insurance. Yet when most investors invest, they invest without insurance. When the stock market crashed, they lost because they had no insurance.

When I invest in real estate I have insurance. If the building burns down, my losses are covered. Even my loss of income is insured.

The biggest losers in the last crash were investors who had their money, uninsured, in retirement plans, plans like the 401(k) in the United States. That is beyond risky. That is foolish.

We all know the markets will crash again, yet most investors invest without insurance.

FAQ
How long did the Great Depression last?

Short Answer
25 years.

Explanation
In 1929 the Dow hit an all-time high of 381. It took till 1954— 25 years—for it to reach 381 again.

This is the problem for those investing for capital gains. This is why gold investors who rushed in late in 1980 to buy gold at $850 an ounce have not yet recovered. This is why baby boomers who were counting on their retirement plans filled with a diversified portfolio of paper assets and their home's appreciation (capital gains) for their retirement are in trouble today.

On October 9, 2007, the Dow hit an all-time high of 14,164. On March 9, 2009, it had fallen to 6,547. Millions of investors lost trillions of dollars. How long will it be before capital-gains investors get their money back?

Today millions of people have their fingers crossed, hoping the Dow keeps climbing. This is not investing. This is gambling. Betting your future on the ups and downs of any market is risky, very risky.

I was taught to diversify differently. I own assets in different asset classes, not just in paper assets. For example, I do invest in oil, but I do not invest in oil company stocks. I do invest in real estate. I do not invest in REITs, Real Estate Investment Trusts, a mutual fund for real estate. I love cash flow, infinite returns, and tax advantages, which is why I generally stay out of paper assets.

Bonds are paper assets. I do not invest in bonds. Rather I borrow the money that bonds create to buy apartment houses, especially when interest rates are low.

When the Fed and central banks are printing money, I save gold and silver, not money. If the banks stop printing money, I will sell gold and silver and go back to cash.

Simply put, I diversify by owning percentages of the different asset classes, not the paper assets (shares, bonds, mutual funds, ETFs) representing the different asset classes.

As Warren Buffett says, "Diversification is protection from ignorance."

The question is, "From whose ignorance—yours, or the stock broker and financial planners selling you the de-worsified portfolio?" Or your real estate broker who tells you your home is an asset and that real estate always goes up in value (capital gains)?

Fin Ed Definition

A mutual fund is already diversified. Generally, a mutual fund is a diversified assortment of stocks, bonds, or other so-called assets. When a person buys a diversified portfolio of mutual funds, in many cases, they are buying the same stocks in different mutual funds. This is not diversification. This is concentration.

7. Debt-Free

I always chuckle when someone says to me, "I am debt-free. My house and car are paid for, and we pay off our credit cards the moment we use them."

Rather than disturb their dream, I say, "Congratulations," and move on. Let them live in their oxymoron.

What I want to say is, "Have you seen the size of the national debt? How can you be debt-free when you and I are paying the principal and interest on nearly $75 trillion in debt? How can you be so naïve?"

In 2010, every U.S. citizen's share of the national debt was $174,000 per person or $665,000 per family.

A Crash of People

The subprime crash of 2007 was caused by excessive debt owed by subprime borrowers.

A Crash of Nations

The next crash will be caused by excessive debt owed by subprime nations. So far, the world has supported the crash of smaller countries, such as the PIIGS (Portugal, Ireland, Italy, Greece, and Spain).

If Germany had not bailed out Greece, the crash would have spread. The first major country to go will probably be Japan.

Why is Japan in trouble? Debt. Japan has the largest percentage of debt-to-GDP ratio of the major world powers. The irony is that

Japan is a highly educated, hardworking, homogenous population, with one of the highest savings rates in the world. In spite of these solid personal work and savings ethics, their government continues to mismanage their economy.

The illusion American leaders promote is that Americans can work hard and produce our way out of these rising mountains of debt, that Americans need to work harder and save more money. This is why President Obama says, "American workers are the most productive workers in the world." It seems he wants American workers to save the U.S. economy when it is the ongoing incompetence of our political and financial leaders that is the true cause of the problem. The people that need financial education the most are our leaders.

Thinking that hard work and thrift will save the U.S. economy is equivalent to a worker earning $10 an hour, believing he can work hard and pay the mortgage of a $2 million home, a Mercedes, a Porsche, a private school for his kids, and save enough for an early secure retirement.

This is the same fantasy millions of Americans, Japanese, Brits, and Europeans and their government leaders are living in. If Japan goes down, crushed by its mountain of debt, the world will follow.

Financial Insanity

Japan is doing the same thing the United States is doing, using debt in an attempt to stimulate their economy. This is no different than a worker using credit cards to pay the interest on their credit cards. During the real estate boom, millions of people refinanced their house to pay off their credit cards and kept using their credit cards. When the entire system crashed, people started losing their homes.

The insanity is that leaders of the Western world are doing the same thing today, using debt to solve a crisis caused by debt.

If Japan does collapse, it may go under by 2015, maybe earlier.

Japan would be followed by England, Europe, the United States, and China. Let's hope it does not happen.

The Baby Boom Bust

In the United States, there are approximately 75 million baby boomers ready to start collecting Social Security and Medicare. Japan, England, France, and Germany have the same problem: baby boomers collecting on promises their countries cannot keep.

If 75 million American baby boomers collect just $1,000 a month in Social Security and Medicare benefits, that is an additional $7.5 billion in monthly payments from the government. Obviously, the printing presses will be running, cranking out checks without money in the bank.

This is why *debt-free* is an oxymoron, even if you are debt-free.

FAQ
How long do we have?

Short Answer
I hope it never happens. But if the biggest countries collapse under mountains of debt, who will be left to save the world? If Japan goes, the crisis will spread to the rest of the world.

Explanation
In 2010, Japan's debt was 200 percent of GDP. The United States is approximately 58.9 percent debt to GDP and growing. England's is 71% and growing.

Fin Ed Definition
Debt-to-GDP ratio is a comparison of what a country owes to what it produces, indicating the country's ability to pay back its debt.
For example, in Japan's case, their GDP is approximately $5 trillion, the fourth largest economy in the world, and their reported debt is approximately $10 trillion. This is approximately $75,000 per person.

Japan's debt-to-GDP ratio is similar to a worker earning $50,000 a year with $100,000 in credit-card debt. To make matters worse, the worker is using credit cards to pay the interest on their $100,000 debt, an action that only increases the debt.

In very simple terms, debt-to-GDP ratio is a country's credit score.

FAQ
Why is debt rising?

Short Answer
Countries are like many people: They spend more than they produce and make promises they cannot afford.

Explanation
The largest growing debt for the United States comes from Social Security and Medicare, aka promises we cannot afford.

FAQ
Were the social promises made by Democrats or Republicans?

Short Answer
Both.

Explanation
Social Security was created under President Franklin Roosevelt, a Democrat, during the last depression.

Medicare was created under President Lyndon Johnson, a Democrat.

Medicare comes in three parts, A, B, and C.

Medicare Part C is one of our largest growing liabilities, and it was created under President George W. Bush, a Republican. It was a multibillion dollar gift to the pharmaceutical industry.

FAQ
Are politicians to blame?

Short Answer
No. The people are.

Explanation
Politicians will say anything and make any promise to get elected.
Once they leave office, the politician receives their paycheck and
medical benefits for life, and the voters are left paying for promises
they cannot afford.

FAQ
How long can this go on?

Short Answer
Not much longer.

Explanation
No fiat currency has ever survived. The U.S. dollar has lost 90 percent
of its purchasing power in forty years. It will not take much time for
it to lose the last 10 percent. There is only so much debt the system
can tolerate.

Time to Take Action

FAQ
What can I do?

Short Answer
Reduce risk.

FAQ
How do I reduce risk?

Short Answer
Take control.

Explanation

The opposite of risk is control. For example, if the brakes on your car went out, you have less control and risk would go up.

FAQ

What do I take control of?

Short Answer

Your education.

Explanation

When we are in school, we have very little control over what we learn and who our teachers are.

For example, at the military academy in New York, I was required to take three years of calculus. Every time I asked my teacher, "Why am I studying calculus?" his reply was, "Because calculus is a requirement for you to graduate."

When I asked, "How will I use three years of calculus in the real world?" his reply was, "I don't know."

In the 40 years since I graduated, I have yet to use any of the calculus I learned. Simple math—addition, subtraction, multiplication, and division—is all I need to build and control my wealth.

If you are going to be a rocket scientist, you need calculus. If you just want to be rich, grade-school math is all that is required.

Earlier I stated that my rich dad advised me to learn three things if I wanted to follow in his footsteps. Those three are:

1. Learn to sell (control income).
2. Learn to invest in real estate (control debt).
3. Learn technical investing (control markets).

These three courses are important for people who want to be in the B and I quadrants. These three courses reduced my risk and increased my control in the B and I quadrants.

FAQ

I understand why selling is important if you want to be an
entrepreneur. I know why using debt to achieve long-term
cash flow is important if you want to invest in real estate.
But why technical investing?

Short Answer

To see the past, present, and future.

Explanation

Technical investors use charts based upon facts to know the past, the
present, and hopefully see the future.

Pictured below is the chart for the price of gold over the past 10 years.

Reprinted with permission

As you can see, gold has been climbing in price for ten years.

Pictured below is the price of gold starting in April 2010.

To me, this shows that gold will climb for a while longer. It is like a climber just about to take on the summit. The steepest part is yet to come. That is the story the chart is telling me. People who do not like gold and look at the same chart would say the bubble has burst and the price will plunge.

This is why I prefer silver. Silver is still sleeping and affordable for everyone, even poor people.

As I write, gold is close to $1,400 and silver is over $30. Gold is hoarded, and silver is consumed. Silver is the sleeper, but you have to do your own research and come to your own conclusions.

What does the future hold? All I do is look at the latest trend of the U.S. dollar, pictured below, and I continue to buy and hold gold and silver.

$USD (US Dollar Index (EOD)) INDX   @ StockCharts.com
1-Oct-2010   Open 78.80 High 78.83 Low 78.06 Close 78.09 Chg -0.63 (-0.80%) ▾

Reprinted with permission

Obviously, charts are always changing as the economy changes, which is why a course on technical analysis is essential.

Charts allow you to see the past and present, and provide you with a better chance of accurately predicting the future. Charts reduce risk and may increase rewards. This is why rich dad recommended that I take classes on technical analysis, or charts, because charts are based upon facts, not opinions.

A Different Focus

My rich dad suggested that I learn to sell, learn to invest in real estate, and learn technical analysis, because I was preparing for the B and I quadrants.

Looking at a financial statement, you will see the difference between E/S and B/I. They focus on different parts of the financial statement, which is why a different education is required.

E's and S's focus on income:

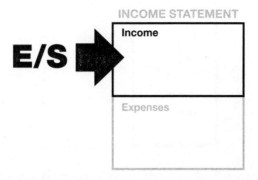

B's and I's focus on assets:

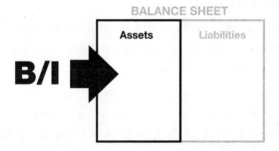

What is Risky?

E's and S's believe investing is risky because they have limited, if any, financial education about assets in the asset column. Investing is not risky. A lack of financial education is very risky.

B's and I's focus on assets which teaches them to manage assets and reduce risk.

Four Different Asset Classes

As a young boy, my rich dad taught me about the four basic asset classes in the asset column. He said, "The more you know about the different asset classes, the more your control goes up and your risk goes down."

There are four basic asset classes in the asset column pictured below.

BALANCE SHEET

Assets	Liabilities
Business	
Real Estate	
Paper Assets	
Commodities	

The ability to sell, manage debt, and analyze market trends is essential to all four asset classes.

Asset Class: Business

The richest people in the world are entrepreneurs such as Bill Gates of Microsoft, Steve Jobs of Apple, Richard Branson of Virgin, and Sergey Brin of Google.

The ability to sell is essential for entrepreneurs. The reason most businesses fail is because the entrepreneur lacks adequate sales skills. In 1974, IBM and Xerox had the best sales training. I was hired by Xerox and was sent to Leesburg, Virginia, for intensive sales training. It took me four years of training to go from last place to first in sales.

I never did well in English in school because I could not write. I still do not write well. Yet, as stated in *Rich Dad Poor Dad*, I am not a "best-writing" author. I am a best-selling author.

Rich dad often said, "Sales equals income." If you want more income, learn to sell.

Asset Class: Real Estate

Real estate is the asset that requires the ability to control debt and manage property and tenants.

In 1973, I took my first real estate-sales course. Today, Kim and I are tens of millions of dollars in debt, debt that produces millions in income, much of it tax-free. In the past year, banks have lowered interest rates which reduces our mortgage payments and increases our profits. Real estate is great because debt and taxes make the investor rich.

Asset Class: Paper Assets

Kim and I rarely invest in paper assets because paper assets offer the least control. When you look at stocks, bonds, or mutual funds, the investor has zero control over income, expenses, assets, and liabilities.

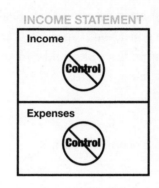

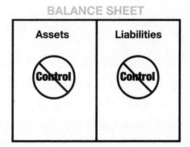

Asset Class: Commodities

Buying gold and silver coins takes the least financial education, yet you still need to know something about the asset class. Gold and silver do go up and down in price. Also, there are many con artists in the gold and silver business, especially today with prices climbing.

Which Asset Class Is Best for You?

FAQ

Which asset class is best for me?

Short Answer

The ones you are interested in.

Explanation

Remember, a business creates most of the truly wealthy people, but a business takes the most financial education. Real estate requires the second-highest financial education. Paper assets are easy to get into, but are the riskiest. Commodities like gold and silver take the least financial education but are not risk-free.

FAQ

Which asset class do most people invest in?

Short Answer

Paper assets.

Explanation

Paper assets are the most liquid, which means they are easy to get into and get out of. Getting into paper assets requires the least financial education, zero sales skills, and zero management skills. All you have to do is go online or call a broker and say, "I want to buy 100 shares of this or sell 100 shares of that." You can train a monkey to buy and sell paper assets.

FAQ

Why don't you invest more in paper assets?

Short Answer

Not enough control.

Explanation

As an entrepreneur, I want control of the income, expense, asset, and liability columns of the financial statement.

If I invest in, let's say, Microsoft, Bill Gates will not take my call. He does not care if I think his expenses are too high or too low. I care. When I invest in oil, I can call the president and he will take my call. When I invest in real estate, I can call Ken McElroy or my manager on duty. When I run my business, I can call anyone in the offices around the world and discuss the business. That is what I mean by control.

This does not mean paper assets are a bad investment. Paper assets make a few people very rich. Paper assets have also lost trillions for unsophisticated investors forced into the stock market by government laws, laws which created pension plans such as the 401(k) in America.

Fin Ed History
In 1974, the U.S. government passed ERISA, the Employee Retirement Income Security Act. This act eventually became known as the 401(k) Act. In simple terms, corporations were no longer willing to pay an employee a paycheck for life. Employees were too expensive, and the United States could not compete with low-wage countries.

Without any financial education, workers throughout the world were forced to become investors. When this happened, the number of financial planners exploded. It was like throwing lambs to a group of lions.

Many schoolteachers, nurses, checkout clerks, and insurance salespeople changed professions and became financial planners. Again, the problem is that most financial planners get their financial education learning to sell in the S quadrant, rather than the I quadrant.

To be fair, I have met a few excellent, very smart, very dedicated financial planners. The problem is that I have met only a few. Most financial planners are in the business to make money. They know how to sell their products, generally paper assets. In fact, most financial planners can only sell the products of the company they work for. Since they do not make money selling other assets, most know little about real estate, oil, taxes, debt, technical analysis, and the historical reasons why the price of gold is going up.

Good financial education is essential for knowing good financial advice from bad advice.

If your financial advisor lost your money, I would not blame the advisor. I would look at myself and ask whether I'm willing to reduce risk by increasing my financial education, which you are doing now.

There are some horrible and stupid financial advisors in the real world. But if you do not know good advice from bad, any advice will do.

FAQ
How does a person make money and reduce risk in paper assets?

Short Answer
Start at the shallow end of the pool. Take classes and practice, aka paper trading.

Commercial Message: Rich Dad suggests playing the *CASHFLOW 202* game, a fun and fantastic way to learn to reduce risk and increase returns with paper assets. You need to understand *CASHFLOW 101* before going on to *202*.

Explanation
In the world of investing, there are always professionals and amateurs. The stock market is a great place for professionals because there are so many amateurs who are forced to be in the deep end of the pool where the sharks wait.

I am not good at paper assets, so it's best I defer to Andy again and let him explain the world from his point of view. He is great at investing in paper assets and is a great teacher. Here's Andy's explanation:

Andy Tanner explains:
When it comes to paper assets, I'd say the biggest differences between amateur investors and professional investors are:
a) how they seek to generate income, and b) how they manage risk. The easier of the two discussions is their approach to managing risk.

In real estate, the battle cry is usually "location, location, location." It seems that in paper assets the battle cry is "diversification, diversification, diversification." In my opinion, in both real estate and paper, the battle cry should be "cash flow, cash flow, cash flow."

Less-sophisticated investors seem more likely to turn to managing risk by what they have been sold as diversification. This brand of diversification is a hope that the winners will outnumber losers at a pace that will achieve financial objectives, outpace inflation, and not be hurt by possible changes in the tax law. But professionals will often seek to manage risk by purchasing contracts. While these contracts cost money, they give the investor the chance to regain some control. While I can't prevent or control a hurricane Katrina, a flood-insurance contract controls the risk associated with the event if it happens.

For example, one investor will simply spread her money around lots of different stocks and hope winners outnumber losers in the long run. Another investor will purchase a contract that gives them the right to sell their stock at a set price, no matter how bad the stock price falls. A put option contract is one simple type of contract that does this.

The discussion of generating income from paper is a little more involved. When an investor plays the *CASHFLOW 202* game, one of the important things that's taught is the difference between an investment that has a goal of producing cash flow and an investment with a goal of producing a capital gain. It's my opinion that amateurs rely more on capital gain, and the professionals tend to seek cash flow.

So, in a nutshell, amateurs often seek to earn their money in paper from capital gains and to manage risk by diversification. The professionals often seek to earn their money with cash-flow strategies and to manage risk by using contracts.

Insurance for Paper Assets

Andy put it very well. In 2007, it disturbed me deeply to watch the stock market crash, knowing the consequences for millions of investors, investors who believed that the stock market always goes up over the long term and that diversification was insurance against losses.

Making matters worse, in 2010, uninsured investors were reentering the market, hoping prices would go up again (capital gains).

Professional investors invest with insurance, even in the stock market.

Again, I turn to Andy to explain how he uses insurance to protect his paper-asset investments.

Andy Tanner explains:

One of the things I purchase on a regular basis is rental insurance. I do this in case my tenants damage my property by accidentally starting a fire, for example. Imagine trying to manage that risk with diversification. It wouldn't make much sense to me to buy a whole bunch of houses and just hope that while some might burn down, most will not.

I like the idea of having a contract that I pay a relatively small amount of money for to protect an asset that is worth a much larger amount of money. Most of us call these types of contracts "insurance." When a person gets in an automobile accident, the first question that is often asked is, "Are you covered?" or "Do you have insurance coverage?"

In the stock market, we don't usually use the word insurance. Instead, we use the word "hedge."

Like insurance, we can protect a relatively large amount of money against loss by spending a relatively small amount of money on a contract, such as a simple put option, as I mentioned above. Many professional investors will spend money on put options during times of uncertainty and when they're faced with events that are beyond their control, such as an earnings report or an announcement by the Federal Reserve. The more risky the situation, the more expensive the contract. In fact, these kinds of contracts can give an investor insight as to how risky the situation is.

An example of this is the credit-default swaps for countries like Greece, Portugal, Ireland, and Spain. Lenders don't want to lend money to all these countries and hope that some pay them back and some won't. They want contracts that protect them against default. Lately, the price of these contracts has been soaring, which tells me things are getting more unstable.

Ireland, Greece Debt Woes Reverse Sovereign Default Swaps Rally

October 29, 2010, 12:32 PM EDT

By Abigail Moses

Oct. 29 (Bloomberg) -- A bondholder showdown in Ireland, slumping Greek tax revenue and political gridlock in Portugal reversed Europe's biggest sovereign debt rally in three months.

The average price of credit-default swaps on Portugal, Italy, Ireland, Greece and Spain rose to 406.5 basis points from 363.5 last week, according to CMA. That's the biggest weekly increase since Aug. 13.

Governments of Europe's so-called peripheral nations are struggling to lower their budget deficits even as they impose public spending cuts and increase taxes. A review of Greece's 2009 budget showed the deficit was above 15 percent of gross domestic product, more than previously estimated, and the nation has "serious tax compliance issues," Finance Minister George Papaconstantinou said this week.

"They need to get out of a deficit spiral," said Tim Brunne, a Munich-based strategist at UniCredit SpA. "It becomes increasingly difficult if you have high debt, and that feeds back again into your deficit and that's a very difficult spiral to get out of."

Credit-default swaps on Greece jumped to 794 basis points today from 671.5 last week, CMA prices show. The contracts pay the buyer face value in exchange for the underlying securities or the cash equivalent should a borrower fail to adhere to its debt agreements. An increase signals deterioration in perceptions of credit quality.

No Negotiations

Swaps on Ireland soared to 474 basis points today from 428 Oct. 22 as the government became locked in a standoff with Anglo Irish Bank Corp. noteholders over who should bear the cost of rescuing the nationalized lender. Alan Dukes, the chairman of the bank, said he wouldn't negotiate with creditors who pledged to block a proposed debt exchange that will impose almost $2 billion of losses.

Portugal climbed to 378 basis points from 343 last week after the government and the country's main opposition party broke off talks on the biggest budget cuts since at least the 1970s, possibly jeopardizing passage of the 2011 plan to tame the euro-region's fourth-biggest deficit.

MORE FROM BUSINESSWEEK

STORY TOOLS

e-mail this story

print this story

Recommend

1 Digg

add to Business Exchange

But a person doesn't need to be a multi-multimillionaire to take advantage of hedging. With a little bit of education, anyone can learn how to use an option contract to protect themselves against loss.

The irony of this idea is that many people label the options market as too risky. In reality, many of the people who purchase options are doing so to reduce their risk. They use the option as a hedge, rather than for speculation. I purchase many options with the idea that I will lose 100 percent of the money I've spent on the option. To me, the context is not much different than the money I spend on insuring my rental property. The income from the rental property pays for the insurance, just as the income from a paper asset will pay for the option that protects it.

Printing Money with Paper Assets

FAQ

Can you print your own money with paper assets? Can I achieve an infinite return on my investment?

Short Answer

Yes.

Explanation

I will let Andy explain, since this is his area of expertise.

Andy Tanner explains:

We know that it is impossible for a stock to actually reach the theoretical number of infinity. However, in the stock market, we can place transactions that can put us at risk for an infinite loss. One example of that is shorting a stock. When we short a stock, we lose money as the stock price goes up. Since there's no limit to how high a stock price can go, shorting a stock is considered to be a transaction that carries infinite risk. So while the stock price will never actually reach infinity, infinity is a concept we must understand for both gain and loss.

Another way to look at infinity is this: As the amount of our own money that we place in an investment approaches zero, the return we receive on that investment approaches infinity. So if we can find a real estate investment that doesn't require any of our own money, we are applying the concept of infinite return. That's one of the reasons why debt, in the real estate world, can make you rich.

With paper assets, we can do this without using any debt at all. That's right: zero debt. And because one of the things that paper assets brings to the table is the ability to scale, this type of investing is available to almost anyone who is willing to obtain the necessary financial education. Again, I want to emphasize that a person does not need to be a multi-multimillionaire to learn about these types of investments.

When Robert asked me to contribute to this chapter and show how to "print money," I thought the easiest way to do it might be to make a very small trade (1,000 shares) and use it as an example that earns between $500 and $600 or so in cash flow. Even though this is the same process my hedge-fund friends apply to millions, we can actually scale it down to someone who just wants to generate their first few hundred dollars from somewhere other than a job. I will use some pictures to illustrate and also use the simple concept of hedging we discussed earlier in the chapter.

In the world of paper assets, an investor can choose to be a buyer of a contract and spend money, or be the seller of a contract and receive money. It's actually a very straightforward concept. Buyers spend money. Sellers receive money.

Robert often mentions the importance of taking a class to learn basic technical analysis. It's the term we use to look at the ups and downs of markets. It's one of the things we can get somewhat familiar with by playing the *CASHFLOW 202* game.

Here is an illustration of the ups and downs of the S&P 500:

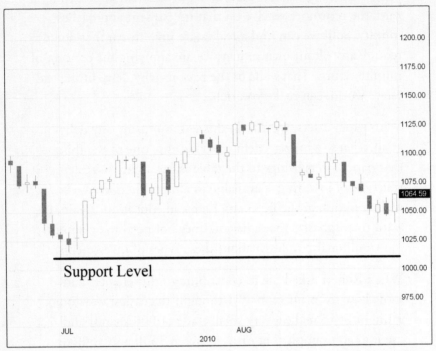

Reprinted with permission

Since there is a strong level of support just above the 1,000 level, an investor might seek to "print some money" by selling a put option contract at, say, the 945 level. But we don't actually call it "printing money." We call it "writing an option."

That simply means that the buyer of the contract would now have "insurance" on the S&P 500 if it were to fall below 945 before the contract expires.

On a financial statement, we can draw a picture of that sale "that puts money in our pocket." It would look something like this:

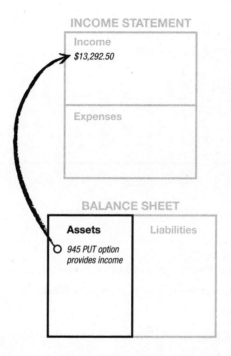

It's interesting to note at this point that a lot of people criticized Robert for saying that "your house is not an asset" because it doesn't put money in your pocket. I could see myself drawing similar criticism for placing a short stock, or a short option, in an asset column. So be it. The fact is, they produce income. On your brokerage statement, it might look something like the picture below. Notice that the adjusted cost is zero, so the adjusted return is infinite (or undefined) when the option expires.

SECURITY	TRANS TYPE	QTY	OPEN	ADJ COST PER SHARE	ADJ COST	CLOSE	ADJ PROCEEDS PER SHARE	ADJ PROCEEDS	ADJ GAIN ($)	ADJ GAIN (%)
SPX Oct 16 2010 945 Put	Exp Short	1,000	8/25/10	$0.00	$0.00	10/18/10	$13.29	$13,292.50	$13,292.50	-

Reprinted with permission

While it can be difficult to predict the direction the market will go, finding a range in which it is likely to reside for a short time—be it up, down, or sideways—is much easier, in my opinion.

Here we see how the market actually moved until expiration.

Reprinted with permission

Of course, when we are the buyer of insurance, it is an expense, and it brings the buyer no money unless our house burns down. The same is true with this put option example. So being the seller of an option is a common way that sophisticated investors make money.

This is actually very similar to one of the ways Warren Buffett has been making money in the market for a long time. As the *Wall Street Journal* reported:

THE WALL STREET JOURNAL | MARKETS

Buffett Scores With Derivatives

by Karen Richardson

Billionaire insurance salesman Warren Buffett has been selling more derivatives recently.

This year, Berkshire Hathaway Inc., the Omaha, Neb., holding company headed by Mr. Buffett, has collected premiums of about $2.5 billion from selling insurance on stock indexes and bonds in the form of derivative contracts, which guarantee payment to the buyer in the event of a specific loss in an underlying entity of the contracts.

Reprinted with permission

Some people mistakenly think that Warren Buffett is against the use of these contracts because he has referred to certain kinds of them as "financial weapons of mass destruction." And, for the uneducated, they probably are. But Buffett actually makes billions and billions from selling them himself. Because there is so little control with paper assets, they carry more risk. So investors will pay lots of money to hedge.

In fact, we can actually use the money we receive for selling put options to buy puts to use as a hedge to control our risk, and still receive a positive cash flow.

That would look like this:

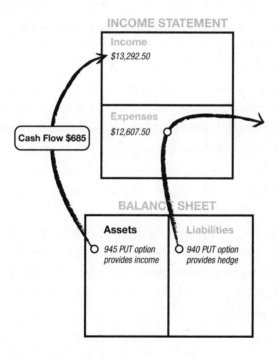

Notice on our statement from the brokerage that we get an infinite return on the options we sold and a 100 percent loss on the put options that we purchased—very similar to the money we might spend for insurance on a house.

To someone who is new to these types of transactions, it may seem like there's a lot to learn. And there is. But with a constant commitment to their financial education, I believe anyone can learn it.

SECURITY	TRANS TYPE	QTY	OPEN	ADJ COST PER SHARE	ADJ COST	CLOSE	ADJ PROCEEDS PER SHARE	ADJ PROCEEDS	ADJ GAIN ($)	ADJ GAIN (%)
SPX Oct 16 2010 945 Put	Exp Short	1,000	8/25/10	$0.00	$0.00	10/18/10	$13.29	$13,292.50	$13,292.50	-
SPX Oct 16 2010 940 Put	Exp Long	1,000	8/25/10	$12.61	$12,607.50	10/18/10	$0.00	$0.00	-$12,607.50	-100.00

Reprinted with permission

I am going to now hand it back over to Robert.

Protection from Robin Hood

As a child, I loved the story of Robin Hood. As I grew up, I realized Robin Hood was a thief. He justified his actions by vilifying the royals and saying, "I steal from the rich to give to the poor." Today, millions of people believe it is okay to steal from the rich and give to themselves.

As the economy worsens and poverty increases, more people will turn into Robin Hoods. Some will turn into felons: breaking into homes, hijacking cars, kidnapping people, and robbing banks. There are others who will steal from you via the court system.

Recently, I had to go to court. A person I did business with in 2005 claimed that I owed him 60 percent of my wealth. Although he has no case, we still had to go to court.

In 2007, he was flying high. Today he is bankrupt and looking for an innovative way to make money, so he put on his Robin Hood costume and we went to court. After the judge told him he had no case, he is now willing to settle for a hundred thousand dollars. The case is still not settled.

FAQ

How do you protect yourself from Robin Hoods?

Short Answer

Use the laws of the rich.

Explanation

There are many ways to protect your wealth, such as a house alarm, insurance, a gun, or a dog.

For centuries, the wealthy have used legal entities such as corporations. For a better explanation of how legal entities are used to protect the wealth of the wealthy, my legal advisor, Garrett Sutton, will take over.

Garrett Sutton explains:

We don't have to get too legal to know that investing involves risk. When investing involves unlimited risk, the chance that out of the blue you'll lose absolutely everything you own, fewer people will invest. But when you can hedge your bets and shield some of your assets, more people will put their money to work.

It started with corporate charters granted by the English Crown in the 1500s. The wealthy and the well-connected were able to take risks that others could not, and the English economy flourished. In time, governments realized that limited-liability entities should offer an equal should offer an equal opportunity for protection.[1] Of course, the face that tax revenues greatly increased with such an expansion of rights certainly helped governments make the right decision.

Today states such as Nevada, Wyoming, and Delaware provide favorable risk-protection laws and affordable fees, and generate huge sums of money for their treasuries. And, in one of the bigger win-wins out there, they allow investors to legally hedge their bets through state-chartered limited-liability entities which has allowed the economy to grow and more taxes to be collected. Much can be explained by examining self-interest.

Ironically, while providing for the good entity choices, governments also offer bad entity choices and don't tell you which ones to use. The paternalistic nanny state so many complain of certainly had not come to entity selection. The government doesn't teach it or warn about it,[2] and they'll let you make the wrong decision.

The bad entity choices, and the ones that offer no protection from claims and thus no minimization of risk, are sole proprietorships and general partnerships. You will not enter into businesses or protect your wealth with these entities. The rich learned this a long time a go. If your advisor advocates using a sole proprietorship or general partnership do what the rich do: Move up to the next level. Get a new advisor who knows how to protect you.

Nevada has the best law on asset-protection trusts. Assets that have been in the trust for over two years cannot be reached by creditors, even with a court order. An example of this structure is as follows:

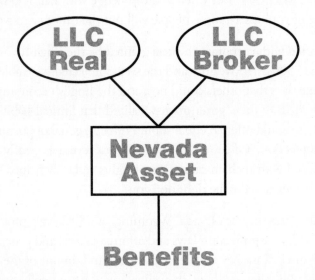

The LLC allows you to manage and protect the property. The asset-protection trust puts up an even bigger wall, protecting you as the beneficiary from creditors.

In setting up an asset-protection plan for clients, I am sometimes asked the question: Won't the government or the IRS be suspicious of this?

My answer involves the history we discussed at the start. Governments encourage asset-protection planning. They allow for the charters, the laws, and the taxation. They want the rich and everyone else to invest and take risks. In turn, they gain significant tax revenue. So do what the government wants: Protect your assets.

In Conclusion

Thank you, Garrett. This has been a long chapter because risk is a massive subject.

The best way to minimize risk is not by avoiding risk and using oxy morons that actually increase risk. The best way to reduce risk is by taking control. And that starts with your financial education. The more you know, the greater control you have over your life and finances.

Risk is real. Accidents, mistakes, and crimes happen every day. One of the reasons the rich get richer is that they take control of their financial education, rather than avoiding risk and believing in job security, saving money, safe investments, fair share, mutual funds, diversified portfolios, and being debt-free—oxymorons that actually increase risk.

Risk is increasing, and it's tied to uncertainty. With terrorism, economic uncertainty, the rise of China, and the decline of the West, risk will increase because uncertainty is increasing.

True financial education gives you more control over risk. And that control over risk is an unfair advantage.

---

1. Petitioning the Crown for a corporate charter was time-consuming and unseemly, and more than a few monarchs cared nothing for "business." But their regents saw it clearly.

2. Perhaps we are not ready to see the following:
   Government Warning: (1) According to the Department of Justice, use of a sole proprietorship may expose all of your assets to the risk of immediate loss. (2) Use of a sole proprietorship impairs your ability to build business credit and may stunt any future economic opportunities.

Chapter Five

UNFAIR ADVANTAGE #5: COMPENSATION

The Rich Don't Work for Money

In *Rich Dad Poor Dad,* rich dad's #1 lesson is, "The rich don't work for money."

This statement bothered many people in 1997 when *Rich Dad Poor Dad* was published and still does today—especially people who believe the rich are money-hungry people. Granted, a few are.

Yet, it is people who work for money who become the money-hungry people, especially in a financial crisis.

FAQ

Why not work for money?

Short Answer

Because money is no longer money.

Explanation

In the old economy, it was possible to work hard and save enough money to enjoy a good life. Once a person retired, they would earn enough interest from their savings to live a comfortable life.

In this new post-crisis economy, not only are interest rates at record-low rates, but the government continues to print trillions in counterfeit money, an action that destroys the purchasing power of your labor and your savings.

Most frightening in the new economy is the compounding interest on trillions of dollars of debt. I do not know how this is sustainable. If interest rates rise, as they did in the 1980s, the world will go bust when U.S. taxpayers say, "Sorry, we can't make the mortgage payment on the national debt this month." When that happens, the real economic crisis will surface.

The power that debt wields over an economy has already occurred in Japan, Latin America, Mexico, Russia, Iceland, Greece, Spain, Italy, Portugal, and Ireland. America, England, and Europe are soon to follow. Welcome to the new economy.

The Three-Legged Stool

In the old economy, financial advisors often spoke of the three-legged stool of retirement. One leg was personal savings, one leg was a company pension, and the third leg was Social Security. The three-legged stool supported the World War II generation, but for millions in the baby-boom generation in the United States, their three-legged stool will have no legs.

FAQ
What happens if I work for money?

Short Answer
The more money you make... the more money you lose.

Explanation
Two things happen for people working for money.

1. They get caught in the cycle of hard work, higher taxes, debt, and inflation. They look like rats in a pet store, running furiously on the wheel to nowhere.
2. They stop working. Many people simply say, "Why work any harder? If I make more money, the government just takes more. Why work if I can't get ahead?"

This is why the rich don't work for money.
In the new economy, a person needs to know how to convert their
phony money into real money as quickly and safely as possible.

This takes financial education, education that will prepare you to
do what the government wants done: things like owning a business
that employs people rather than the employee, providing housing
rather than buying a house, producing oil rather than burning oil,
and producing food rather than eating food. In countries all over the
world, governments reward *producers* and punish *consumers* who work
for money.

More Money Does Not Make You Rich

I can remember in the 1950s, when my poor dad earned $300
a month, or $3,600 a year. His income barely covered the living
expenses for a family of six. He worked very hard but was always
broke, spending more than he earned, and our family struggled.
He could not get ahead, so he went back to school for advanced
degrees that would enable him to earn more money.

In the 1960s, his career took off, receiving promotion after
promotion, climbing the ladder inside the educational system of
Hawaii. By 1968, he was earning $65,000 a year as Superintendent of
Education for the state, which was a lot of money then. The problem
was that even with more money, my dad was still broke. He bought a
new house in an expensive neighborhood, a new car, and still had the
expenses of kids in college. His income went up, but so did his lifestyle
expenses. He had no assets except for a little money in savings.

In the early 1970s, he ran for Lt. Governor and lost. In his mid
fifties, he was out of work and even more broke. If not for Social
Security and a small pension, he would have been destitute.

When the dollar went off the gold standard in 1971, the biggest
financial boom in world history began, but my dad was not a part
of it. Although he held a PhD in education, his education had not
prepared him for the real world of money. He saw the world from the
E and S quadrants and knew nothing of the B or I quadrants.

As his friends grew richer, my dad grew angry and bitter. As his anger grew, so did his belief that rich people were greedy people.

Today, millions of people are in the same shoes as my poor dad. Many are well-educated, hardworking people, but they are falling behind, rather than getting ahead in this crisis. They fall behind because they work for money and save money.

Congratulations! You're a Trillionaire!

We know the world is printing money. The world prints money in good economies and bad economies. The question is: How much money is being printed?

If the United States is printing trillions of dollars, how much is the rest of the world printing? Perhaps a better question is: What will trillions in printing-press money do to you? Will trillions of dollars make you richer, or poorer?

If the financial turmoil of the past few years leads us into hyperinflation, there will be more millionaires, billionaires, and even trillionaires. You might be one of them.

Ironically, in this brave new world, there are already many trillionaires, but they are broke. For example, if you moved to Zimbabwe today, you could be a trillionaire in Zimbabwe dollars.

In fact, if you want to be a trillionaire, all you have to do is go online and buy a Zimbabwe trillion-dollar bill and you can go around telling your friends, "I'm a trillionaire."

You would be a trillionaire, but you'd still be broke. Welcome to the new economy.

I carry a *one-hundred-trillion* Zimbabwe note in my wallet. Numerically, that is $100,000,000,000,000. I carry it to remind me that one hundred trillion Zimbabwe dollars may buy me an egg in Zimbabwe, but only if the egg is on sale.

Too *much* money is the trap of the new economy. In spite of trillions of dollars in the U.S. economy, millions of Americans are broke or will soon be broke.

FAQ

If the rich do not work for money, what do they work for?

Short Answer

Assets that produce cash flow in good economies or bad.

Explanation

Rather than save money in a bank or a retirement plan filled with paper assets, it is important to convert those dollars into real assets: assets that retain value, produce cash flow, and offer tax incentives.

FAQ

What makes you so sure your assets are safe assets?

Short Answer

They produce cash flow in good economies and bad economies, with tax incentives.

Explanation

Throughout history, paper money has come and gone. There was the Continental during the Revolutionary War and the Confederate dollar during the Civil War.

Although both currencies collapsed and became worthless, there was still an economy with people working, buying, selling, and trading. In other words, the money became worthless, but the economy kept going.

Many people have become extremely wealthy during financial collapses. Great assets become available for next to nothing. The problem is that people who were trained to look for a job, like my poor dad, cannot tell the difference between assets or liabilities.

I invest in assets that are essential to the economy. I invest in apartment buildings because people need a roof over their head. Most people would rather pay rent than live under a bridge. The government also gives rent subsidies for people without money. If the economy collapses, the government will most likely print money and give money (even if it is worth less and less) to the owners of the apartment houses. With this inflated money from the government, I will pay off my millions in debt with counterfeit money. If the economy collapses, the government will help me pay off my assets simply because the government does not want millions of people on the streets.

I invest in oil because oil keeps the world running, fed, and warm. And I invest in gold and silver because, when governments print money, gold and silver retain their intrinsic value.

There are many different types of assets that are essential to the economy. Find the ones that interest you.

FAQ
How do you know what is important to the economy?

Short Answer
Look at financial statements, especially the expense column.

Explanation
When you look at a person's financial statement, if they have one, you can see what is important to them and their personal economy. Their personal economy is what they must spend money on. A few examples are:

INCOME STATEMENT

Income

Expenses
Taxes: to stay out of jail
Shelter: a roof over their head
Food: without food, cannibalism is next
Fuel: we need to keep moving and warm
Clothing: most look better with clothes on
Communication: cell phones
Transportation: humans need to get to work
Entertainment: recreation, movies and TV
Education: for economic survival

My asset column:

BALANCE SHEET

Assets	Liabilities
Education company Apartment houses Resort with 5 golf courses Commercial buildings Oil Intellectual property Gold and silver Solar business	

FAQ

Can you tell a rich person from a poor person by looking at their financial statement?

Short Answer

Yes.

Explanation

That is why your banker asks for your financial statement, not your report card. When you look at a person's financial statement, you can tell what is important to that person. You can also predict the person's future.

Poor people focus only on the expense column. They earn enough to survive day to day with a roof over their heads, food on the table, gas in the car, and clothes on their backs. It is not a matter of how much they make. It is what they think is important. There are many people who make a lot of money, but spend it all through the expense column. They live paycheck to paycheck, even if they make a lot of money. They have no future because they live for today.

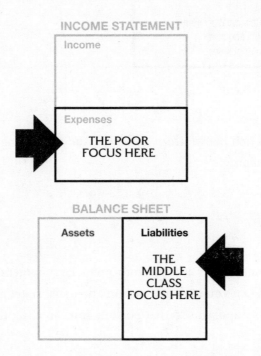

The middle class focuses on the liabilities column. They want liabilities that improve their lifestyle. For the middle-class lifestyle, looking rich is more important than being rich. They want a bigger house, cars, fine food, vacations, education, and life's luxuries... all paid for with debt. They spend more money than they make, and sink deeper and deeper into debt. Rather than buy an apartment house, they buy a bigger house in a better neighborhood that puts them in a better school district. If they invest, they turn their money over to financial planners because they would rather enjoy life than take classes and learn how to manage their own wealth.

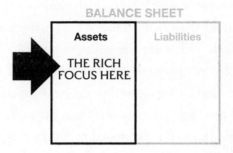

The rich focus on the asset column. They know if they focus on assets first, expenses and liabilities will be handled.

In the new economy, if you do not get your money into the asset column, converting your money into assets that cash flow, you will probably work hard for money all your life.

We Do Not Live Below Our Means

Most financial advisors recommend living below your means. This is good advice for the poor and middle class. It is not good advice for people who want to be rich. Kim and I do not live below our means. We believe living below our means only depresses our spirit.

So rather than live below our means, we invest in education and assets. For example, when we were building The Rich Dad Company, we took classes almost every weekend, learning as much as we could about business in the new economy. We did the same for real estate, technical trading, and commodities.

Today when we want a new liability, maybe a new car or vacation house, all we have to do is acquire or develop an asset first, and that asset will pay for the liability.

A year ago, in the midst of the financial chaos, I wanted a new Ferrari. When I told Kim what I was going to buy, she did not say, "You can't have a new Ferrari. We can't afford it." Nor did she say, "Why do you need a Ferrari? You already have a Lamborghini, Porsche, Bentley and a Ford truck." And she didn't say, "Which car are you going to sell?"

She does not say those words because she knows a new liability will make us richer. Rather than remind me of how many cars I already have, she simply said, "What are you going to invest in?" In other words, what asset are you going to buy that will pay for the liability?

I had already found a new oil well project and invested in the well. When the oil well produced, the income from the well's production paid for the Ferrari. The well is estimated to produce oil for about 20 years. The Ferrari will be paid for long before that oil runs dry.

Kim is happy because she has a new asset, and I am happy because I have a new Ferrari.

Our rule is simple: *Assets buy our liabilities.* Rather than live below our means, we expand our means by focusing on the asset column. Over the years, I have written books, bought a mini-warehouse, and subdivided land to buy liabilities. Some of the liabilities, such as the cars, are long gone, but the assets still provide cash flow. Our liabilities inspire us to become richer.

We also forbid ourselves from saying, "I can't afford it," or "You can't have this or that." We know we can afford anything we want if we acquire assets first. Knowing how to create or acquire assets is why the rich do not work for money.

FAQ
But if you're acquiring assets for cash flow, aren't you still working for money?

Short Answer
Yes, but there are differences. The difference is why the rich get richer, regardless of the economy.

Explanation
Rather than work for money, the rich follow the Laws of Compensation.

The Laws of Compensation

The following section explains three different variations on the Laws of Compensation. To be better compensated, you must follow these laws.

Law of Compensation #1
Reciprocity: Give, and you shall receive.
I learned this law long ago in Sunday school. As obvious as it is, when it comes to money, many people seem to forget this law. They want to receive, but not give, or give only after they receive.

Many people want to be paid more and do less. My poor dad was one of those people. As head of the teachers' union of Hawaii, he worked hard to secure more pay and less work for his teachers. I remember a fight he took on, demanding that teachers teach fewer students for more pay, with more days off and better benefits. To my poor dad, this made sense.

To my rich dad, my poor dad's philosophy violated one of the laws of compensation. Rich dad believed in giving more if you want to receive more.

It always seemed strange to me that many people thought my rich dad was greedy and my poor dad was right in fighting for higher pay and less work for his teachers.

When I graduated from the Merchant Marine Academy at Kings Point, New York, I joined a non-union company, Standard Oil, because I did not want to join the MM&P (Masters, Mates, and Pilots), a professional union for ships' officers. I would have made more money as a union member, but being around my poor dad and his friends, teachers' union officials, I could not subscribe to the union philosophy. In my opinion, the concept of wanting to work less and be paid more ultimately makes everyone poorer, regardless of the amount of money they earn.

One of the reasons there are fewer U.S. cargo ships today and fewer jobs on those ships is because union wages forced shipping companies to move their operations to countries with lower wage scales. One reason why General Motors is in trouble is because the union leaders were stronger than the company leaders. Today, the true cost of unionized labor in the U.S. auto industry is millions of jobs lost, factories moving overseas, and a weaker economy.

This does not mean I am anti-union. Unions have done a lot of good for workers, protecting them from cruel and greedy business owners. Unions gave us the two-day weekend. I respect a person's right to choose their work affiliations and philosophy. When I graduated from the academy, I chose to be non-union. I made my choice because I would rather focus on giving more to receive more, rather than working less and earning more.

Kim becomes richer every year because every year she produces more. In 1989, she started with one rental house. Today, she has over 3,000 rental units. Today she earns more because she provides more housing for more people. In ten years, she may have 20,000 units and she should earn more because she follows the law of compensation. I know some people may say Kim is greedy. I know my poor dad would.

From my rich dad's point of view, Kim is being generous because she obeys the first law of compensation: Give, and you shall receive.

The law of reciprocity also works in reverse. If you cheat people, people will give back to you what you gave them.

This is what happened to Bernie Madoff. He took people's money and wound up in jail. He got what he deserved.

Unfortunately, many of the biggest crooks do not get caught. Some of them are still running the economy.

Law of Compensation #2
Learn to give more.

Most people go to school to learn how to earn money, but only for themselves and their family. Few people go to school to learn how to produce more and produce more for more people.

Most people go to school to become E's and S's. The problem with the left side of the quadrant is that the number of people I can serve is limited. For example, when I graduated from Kings Point, I could work for only one company, Standard Oil, as an employee. Most people in the S quadrant—a medical doctor, for example—can only work on one patient at a time.

The reason I chose to follow my rich dad into the B and I quadrants was because my success would serve more people. The more people I could serve, the more I earned.

When a person is successful in serving more people, taxes and debt also swing to their favor. This is why debt and taxes make people on the B and I side of the quadrant rich.

If you focus on making money just for yourself, or improving life only for yourself and your family, then taxes and debt work against you.

One reason why so many people are limited financially is because they went to school and learned to work for money on the E and S side of the quadrant, rather than learn to serve more people on the B and I side.

Law of Compensation #3
Leverage the power of compounding financial education.
The more you learn on the B and I side, the more you'll earn. Over time, as your education compounds, so do your returns.
In other words, you earn more and more with less and less effort.

This is the true power of financial education.

To better understand the Law of Compensation #3, a person needs to understand that the true power in education is not found in a classroom, seminar, books, report cards, or diplomas.

Simply put, "You can *teach* a person to fish, but you cannot force a person to *learn* to fish." There are two important points related to this statement:

1. The power of education is unleashed after you leave school, take a class, seminar, or read a book and begin applying your education.

    This is why medical doctors go to four years of college, four years of medical school, and then become interns or resident doctors for another four to eight years. Throughout this process they gain real-life experience before becoming real doctors.

    I did not become a ship's officer until after I left the academy. And I did not become a pilot until I had finished two years of flight school. I did not become a competent combat pilot until I was in Vietnam for six months. Incompetent pilots were often dead in the first two months.

    People who have no financial education often fail. Rather than take classes on entrepreneurship or investing, they begin trading stocks, flipping real estate, or become entrepreneurs. Then they wonder why they failed or failed to produce extraordinary results. If they fail, many just quit, blaming something or someone for their failure.

As you may recall from a previous chapter, I stated that in 1973 when my flying career was over, I signed up for real estate-investment classes and sales training with Xerox.

Today people will say to me, "Can I take you to lunch? I want to pick your brains on investing in real estate." It makes me sick to see people so naïve about financial education. Becoming financially educated is not something you do over lunch.

I also have had financial morons tell me, "I have bought and sold a number of personal residences. I know how to invest in real estate."

There is a massive difference between buying a home and buying 300-unit apartment houses. Success or failure lies in the power of financial education. Taking a three-day seminar gave me the fundamentals to become a real estate investor, an investor who uses debt to acquire wealth.

While the fundamentals are the same for a single rental property or a 300- unit apartment house, the difference in profitability is found in education and years of experience.

My poor dad failed in his first and only business venture, an ice-cream franchise. In his mind, it was the franchisor that cheated him. In my opinion, it was his lack of entrepreneurial education and his inexperience that cost him two years of his life and his life savings.

The strange thing about people who did well in school, like my dad, is that they respect academic education, but fail to respect financial education. They seem to think that, just because they hold a PhD or are an attorney, accountant or medical doctor, business and investing should be easy for them.

To me this is academic arrogance. It is also very expensive arrogance.

2. Learning also compounds. The true abundance of money is found in the power of compounding financial education.

   In other words, the more you learn about money in the B and I quadrants, the more money you'll make.

Education's Failure

Pictured below is the Cone of Learning. It was developed by Edgar Dale in 1969.

Cone of Learning

After 2 weeks we tend to remember		Nature of Involvement
90% of what we say and do	Doing the Real Thing	Active
	Simulating the Real Experience	
	Doing a Dramatic Presentation	
70% of what we say	Giving a Talk	
	Participating in a Discussion	
50% of what we hear and see	Seeing it Done on Location	Passive
	Watching a Demonstration	
	Looking at an Exhibit Watching a Demonstration	
	Watching a Movie	
30% of what we see	Looking at Pictures	
20% of what we hear	Hearing Words	
10% of what we read	Reading	

Source: Cone of Learning adapted from Dale, (1969)

The Cone of Learning illustrates the effectiveness of various methods of learning by measuring retention.

You may notice that the most impactful way to learn is illustrated at the top of the cone: simulation and doing the real thing. The least meaningful way to learn is at the bottom of the cone: reading and lecture.

In flight school, pilots were trained extensively on simulators. Once we were competent on simulators, we flew the real aircraft. Kim and I created the *CASHFLOW* game as a simulator. The game allows players to make as many mistakes as possible with play money, not real money.

Cone of Learning

After 2 weeks we tend to remember		Nature of Involvement
90% of what we say and do	Doing the Real Thing	Active
	Simulating the Real Experience	
	Doing a Dramatic Presentation	
70% of what we say	Giving a Talk	
	Participating in a Discussion	
50% of what we hear and see	Seeing it Done on Location	Passive
	Watching a Demonstration	
	Looking at an Exhibit Watching a Demonstration	
	Watching a Movie	
30% of what we see	Looking at Pictures	
20% of what we hear	Hearing Words	
10% of what we read	Reading	

Source: Cone of Learning adapted from Dale, (1969)

There are CASHFLOW clubs all over the world that teach and support people on their path to becoming entrepreneurs and investors, just as the military uses simulators to train military pilots.

A word of caution: Many people play the *CASHFLOW* game once or twice and think they are seasoned investors. Once again, this is arrogance in action.

CASHFLOW clubs will allow you to move on to focus on one of the four asset classes–entrepreneurship and business, real estate, paper assets, or commodities. Then we advise continuing your education, hiring a coach to guide you through your real-life process. The process of investing time to become a better investor or entrepreneur before investing or starting a business with your life savings will help increase your chances of success.

The more important and risky the venture is, the more important games and simulations are in the learning process. That's why professional athletes practice more than play, actors rehearse more than act, and why doctors and lawyers call their businesses a "practice."

The power of compounding education is staggering. Most of us have heard about the power of compounding interest rates. Many of us know that mutual funds profit via the power of compounding expenses. And most of us are very aware of America's compounding national debt.

The Power of Learning

To better explain the power of compounding learning, I will use the game of golf as a metaphor. When a person first takes up the game of golf, the process can be painful, ugly, and frustrating. The new golfer puts in a lot of time and effort for very little in return. Many people quit after the first lesson.

But if they stick with the learning process—take lessons, hire a coach, practice, play eighteen holes three to four days a week, and enter tournaments on weekends—in a few years they are likely to beat most golfers, even golfers with more natural talent.

To truly develop their talents, they would have to increase their dedication to learning.

In the world of professional golfers, the difference between the top 20 money winners and the top 125 golfers is less than two strokes. In other words, the top 20 make millions, and the next 100 golfers earn a comfortable living.

The game is the same. And the difference is not just natural talent. The difference is in dedication to learning to become the best. This is an example of the Third Law of Compensation: the power of compounding education.

Education is not a class, a course, or a few lessons. True education is a process. True education can sometimes be a *painful* process, especially at the start when it's hard work with little in return.

While Tiger Woods may not be a good example of faithfulness in marriage, he is a good example of success in golf. Tiger dropped out of Stanford in 1996 to become a professional golfer at the age of 20. The moment he turned pro, he signed endorsement deals for $40 million with Nike and $20 million with Titleist. Not a bad start for a college dropout.

Some might say he is naturally gifted and an overnight success. He may be naturally gifted, but he was not an overnight success. It took time, dedication, and sacrifice to develop his talents. More important than the age he turned pro is the age at which he started his golf career.

When Tiger was a baby, his dad created a driving range in his garage with a carpet and a net. Before Tiger could walk, he would sit in his high chair and watch his dad hit practice balls into the net.

When he was nine months old, his dad sawed off a golf club so Tiger could hit balls into the same net. When he was 18 months old, Tiger began going to the golf course with his dad and hit buckets of balls on the driving range.

At the age of three, he shot a 48 for nine holes at the Navy Golf Club in California. When he was four, his dad hired a coach for Tiger. At six, he began to play in junior contests. And in1984, at the age of eight, he won the 9-10 boys' event at the Junior World Golf competition.

You get my point.

Success takes an investment in time, dedication, and sacrifice. This is true education. It is a process. For most successful people, there is no such thing as an "overnight success."

My rich dad constantly said, "Success requires sacrifice." He also said, "Most people are not rich because they want money without sacrifice."

The reason so few people make it over to the B and I side of the CASHFLOW Quadrant is because life is easier on the E/S side, at least it may seem that way in the beginning. For most people on the E/S side, life will get harder in the new economy, especially as they grow older. And long-term success also requires strong legal, ethical and moral character, as Tiger is finding out the hard (and expensive) way.

Infinite Returns

Infinite returns are the result of obeying Law of Compensation #3.

When Kim started out in 1989 with her 2-bedroom/1-bath house, she worked really hard just to make $25 a month in net cash flow. Twenty years later, she works less and makes much more money — often infinite returns, which means *money for nothing*. Even in this economic crisis, her wealth is accelerating, making more money with much less effort, because infinite returns are the result of the 3rd law of compensation.

Smarter and Better Friends

One more aspect of Law of Compensation #3 is smarter and better friends. When financial intelligence increases, you also start to meet smarter people. When you meet smarter people, you are invited into investments that are called "insider" investments. These are investments that never make it to market. The investments are so good that the investment does not need to be advertised or sold. Someone makes a phone call, and the investment is off the market.

The resort and golf-course investment that Kim and I have was an insider investment. The moment the property went into foreclosure, the banker called just four people and the property was gone.

This is another example of the power of compounding financial education. If Kim and I were dishonest, immoral, or illegal, we would never have been invited into the partnership. A good reputation is also an unfair advantage.

The Power of Financial Education

Obeying the laws of compensation allowed Kim to retire at 37. I retired at 47. Obeying the laws granted us our financial freedom, something fewer people will achieve in the brave new world of the new economy.

Kim and I founded The Rich Dad Company only after we achieved our freedom. Before we talked or wrote about our freedom, we had to pressure-test our freedom. We wanted to find out if our financial education was real and could survive the ups and downs of the economy.

I would say our freedom survived because we obeyed the laws of compensation. We remembered to give more if we wanted more in return. We continued to learn how to give more from the B and I quadrants. And we knew we had to keep learning and practicing, improving our skills in the B and I quadrants.

FAQ

But didn't your rich dad give you a head start? Isn't that your unfair advantage?

Short Answer

Yes and no.

Explanation

My rich dad did not give me anything. He simply showed me the way. At the age of nine, playing *Monopoly*, I knew the difference between assets and liabilities. But I still had to take classes and learn, turning my education into real assets.

What gave me my unfair advantage was financial education, applied to real life.

The greatest unfair advantage that Kim and I have is that we do not stop learning. We attend classes and apply what we learn. We know that if want more, we need to learn how to give more. The more we give, the more tax breaks and low-interest loans we receive. We know if we give others a better life, we will receive a better life in return.

FAQ

Don't most people attend financial courses to make money only for themselves?

Short Answer

Yes and no.

Explanation

It is very important to learn to take care of yourself. There are too many people who want to save the world but cannot save themselves. If you cannot save yourself, you are less effective in the world.

When I was young, I learned, "God helps those who help themselves." Too many students leave school wanting to help people, but cannot help themselves. If you want to save the world, learn to save yourself first. Then go save the world.

Time to Change Careers

In 1981, I had the privilege of studying with Dr. R. Buckminster Fuller at a weekend conference in the mountains of California. For those not familiar with Dr. Fuller's work, he is often referred to as "The Planet's Friendly Genius." He is the inventor of the geodesic dome and hundreds of other inventions, all dedicated to making the world a better place.

During one of his talks, he said something that changed my life. At the time I was flat broke, having lost my first big business, the nylon-and-Velcro wallet business. I knew what to do but I was struggling. Something was wrong. Sitting there, listening to one of our world's greatest geniuses, I realized what I had forgotten. Listening to him, I realized I was disobeying the Laws of Compensation.

That morning, Dr. Fuller said to the group, "I do not work for money. I have dedicated my life to the service of others." Speaking on principles that govern the world, he said, "The more people I serve, the more effective I become."

His simple words hit me like a lightening bolt. It dawned on me that I was struggling, as my business was struggling, because I was only thinking about making money for myself. I knew it was time for me to change careers, again.

A few months later, I began training to become a teacher, a teacher of entrepreneurship who would follow the principles taught by Dr. Fuller, principles that follow the laws of compensation.

I had a hard time deciding to become a teacher because I really did not like school or most of my teachers. Also, all the teachers I knew were poor. Finally, I resolved my decision to teach by committing to follow the Laws of Compensation and focus on serving more and more people rather than just making money.

The unfair advantage I had over most teachers was that I was an entrepreneur. I knew I could build a business as an educational entrepreneur, outside the traditional school system.

Two years later in 1984, after much practice teaching, often holding seminars that no one came to, I sold my wallet business and took a leap of faith. The moment I made my commitment, I met Kim. When I told her what I was up to, she said she wanted to join me on this new adventure.

Although we had no money, we held each other's hand and took our leap of faith together. I would never have made it without Kim.

In some of our books, I write about the fact that Kim and I were homeless for a time, sleeping in a borrowed car, living in friends' basements or living rooms, while we learned to be teachers.

For five years, we had our faith tested. For five years, it was extremely difficult selling enough seats to our classes to cover business expenses and our living expenses too. After five years, the business picked up and we expanded with offices throughout Australia, Canada, Singapore, New Zealand and throughout the United States.

In 1994, ten years after taking our leap of faith, Kim and I were financially free.

In 1996, following the Laws of Compensation, Kim and I created our board game *CASHFLOW*. We created the game so we could serve more people, teaching people the same financial lessons my rich dad taught me.

In 1997, *Rich Dad Poor Dad* was published. This was a monumental effort because I do not like to write. I flunked out of high school twice because I did not like to write. Yet I wrote that book because I was following the Laws of Compensation with my focus on serving more people, rather than simply making money.

In the year 2000, *Rich Dad Poor Dad* made the *New York Times* best-seller list. It was the only self-published book on the list.

Also in 2000, Oprah Winfrey called and, after one hour on *Oprah* with a woman who is trusted and respected around the world, I went from being a virtual unknown to a player on the world stage.

All Kim and I were doing was following the Laws of Compensation and focusing on serving more people. Today, although we have more than enough money, we keep working and our income from our assets continues to grow. We know it's because we're leveraging our unfair advantage in obeying the Laws of Compensation.

In Closing

I write this book because there is simply too much greed in the world. For this financial crisis to end, we need more generous people.

I write to encourage good people like you to be students of financial education, take care of yourself financially, and focus on being generous with your God-given gifts.

As Dr. Fuller reminded me in 1981, it is by being generous that we find our God-given gifts and our God-given genius.

A CASE FOR CAPITALISM

Capitalism has come under severe attack during this financial crisis. Many people believe capitalists are greedy, corrupt, and evil. Granted, many are.

Yet, if you look at what *true* capitalists do, *true* capitalists only profit if and when they make life better, often saving us time and money. For example, the Wright Brothers were the first to fly, but it took capitalists to build an airline industry, making flying safe and affordable for the masses. Today, I am happy to pay for an airline ticket because flying is easier, faster, and a lot less painful than walking, which we all would be doing if not for capitalists.

The same is true for using my cell phone. I am able to do business anywhere in the world, even while on vacation. I am happy to pay for the use of my cell phone because it makes my life easier and makes me richer.

General Electric, founded by Thomas Edison, not only makes life better through electricity, but also extends life through medical technology. I gladly pay for the benefits that GE medical products bring to my life.

And what would I do without my Apple computer? I might never have written *Rich Dad Poor Dad* if not for Steve Jobs making the computer simple enough for a non-techie like me to use. The few dollars I spend on my computer make me millions of dollars each year.

And my Ferrari, Bentley, Ford, or Porsche would be useless if the government did not tax car owners to build and repair our roads.

I believe you get my point. While it is true that there are greedy, crooked, lazy people who exploit the capitalist system, they are not true capitalists. They are simply greedy, crooked, and lazy people.

This financial crisis was caused by corruption at the highest levels of government and business. Like a cancer, legalized corruption eats away at the moral fiber of the world. Men and women of power, craving more power, sell their souls to glorify their egos, destroying lives and bleeding the wealth from people they are supposed to serve.

In world governments, we have too many professional politicians. Many "public servants" serve without any real-world business experience, running the biggest business in the world—the business of government. No wonder government is corrupt.

While corrupt and incompetent business and political leaders have damaged the economy, I believe one of the biggest reasons for this financial crisis is an obsolete educational system. In the United States, the more we spend on education, the worse the system gets.

One problem with the school system is the failure to focus on true capitalism. Hence, we have corrupted capitalism and corrupted governments running the world. In schools, there is a subtle socialist agenda, a subtle undercurrent implying "the rich are greedy."

In Marxist theory, the proletariat is a class of capitalist society that does not have ownership of the means of production. All they have to sell is their labor for a wage or salary. Proletarians are wage-workers, trained—like Pavlov trained his dogs—to work for money.

Our school system produces this class of capitalism, the proletariat class, a wage earner, a person who leaves school looking for a job. Many will never own anything of value, and many will die with nothing, simply because our schools, while resenting the rich, produce the workers they claim the rich exploit.

A job is not an asset. You cannot own a job. You cannot pass your job on to your kids.

Money is not an asset. Today, money is debt and is rapidly being devalued with more national debt.

Your home is not an asset. You are the asset. Every month,

homeowners send checks to the bank, tax department, insurance, and utility companies.

Your retirement plan is not an asset. It is an unfunded liability. Your retirement savings go to the rich who use your money to acquire their assets—real assets.

Students who leave school, looking for a high-paying job, soon fly into the web of capitalism, not because capitalism is necessarily evil, but because the educational system fails to prepare students for the real world. Without financial education, students are trained to be the victims of capitalism. The school system's belief that "the rich are greedy" becomes a self-fulfilling prophecy.

As I've often stated, true capitalists are generous. They produce a lot and receive a lot. Could it be the school system that is really the greedy party?

Marx envisioned a war between the proletariat and the bourgeoisie, the capitalist class, since workers naturally wish their wages to be as high as possible, while the bourgeoisie, the capitalists, wish for wages to be as low as possible.

In the brave new world of the new economy, in the ongoing war for high wages versus low wages, the capitalist class is winning. The capitalists win because it is easy to move production to lower-wage nations. Technology also reduces the number of workers needed to run a business. Production goes up, labor costs go down, and capitalists win.

The world is changing rapidly. The school systems are not. Schools continue to teach people to be proletarians, to leave school in search of a high-paying job. This is financial suicide.

Always remember: A job is not an asset, nor is money an asset, nor is a home an asset. The worker's savings in their retirement plan is only a source of cash for true capitalists. When markets crash, as they always do, the workers lose, and the capitalists win.

Remember, in Marxist theory, the proletariat is a class of capitalist society that does not have ownership of the means of production. In the new economy, where money is no longer real money, the working class works for nothing. They have no assets.

As an employer, I occasionally interview potential employees looking for a job. Sadly, most are focused on only wages and benefits: "How much will you pay me?" "What are my benefits?" "What are the hours?" "How much time off can I have?" "How fast can I get promoted?"

No one has ever asked: "What is the mission of this company?" "What problem is the company solving?" "What can I learn from working here?"

Rather than ask socially responsible questions, they ask questions about money and working conditions. They ask questions from a proletariat's frame of mind.

This working-class programming begins when parents say to their child: "Go to school to get a high-paying job," or "Go to school and become a lawyer, doctor, or web designer. If you have a profession, you will always have something to fall back on."

Remember rich dad's #1 rule: The rich don't work for money.

Home is where proletariat programming begins. Working-class parents want their kids to become higher-educated working-class people, people who ultimately work for the ultra rich.

When a child enters school, the teachers (who are also from the proletariat class of capitalism, a class that does not own production) continue the programming by saying, "If you do as I tell you and get good grades, you will beat your classmates to that high-paying job."

Once the child enters college, beating out many of their lesser classmates, the teachers continue with their working-class dogma, saying, "If you have a master's degree or a PhD, your resume will look better. The higher your degree, the better your chances of getting that high-paying job."

Pavlov caused his dogs to salivate by ringing a bell. Our education system rings the school bell, chiming the promise of a high-paying job. All someone has to say is "high-paying job," and people start lining up.

If a person "wins" by getting that job and beating out the lesser job candidates, they are only too happy to agree to have their taxes deducted from their paycheck—so the government gets paid before they do.

Once the government is assured of being paid, the new employee agrees to send a portion of their paycheck to a mutual-fund company, investing in their retirement, which means the rich get paid next.

In the United States, if a worker refuses to invest in a company-sponsored retirement plan made up of mutual funds, the employee loses their matching contribution from their employer. In other words, "If you do not pay the Wall Street bankers, we do not have to pay you."

Many employees naïvely believe the matching contribution comes from their employer. The naïve employee does not realize that the matching contribution was his or her money in the first place. If the employee refuses to invest via a payroll-investment plan, the employer saves money.

This is how much power Wall Street has over our government and labor laws, laws that labor unions endorse. Talk about corruption.

As soon as their new job is secure, the new worker begins to save a little money to buy their dream home because they know, "Your home is an asset and your largest investment."

Few people realize that the mortgage, and the homeowner who pays the mortgage, are the real assets.

The new member of the working class is now transferring his or her money into the pockets of the bourgeoisie through the agents of the capitalist class: the bankers, real estate agents, stockbrokers, financial planners, and politicians.

The bourgeoisie isolate their world from the world of the working class via the education system. In other words, the educational system is being used as the primary agent of the so-called "greedy rich" whom educators despise.

This is why there is no true financial education in schools.

Get Off the Plantation

My poor dad became a teacher because he was a product of the plantation system of Hawaii. His father, my grandfather, came over on a boat from Japan to work in the sugar and pineapple fields of Hawaii.

My grandfather married my grandmother, whose family had made the crossing a generation earlier in the 1800s. My grandmother's parents still worked on the plantation when she married my grandfather.

My grandfather wanted nothing to do with life on the plantation. As soon as he was off the boat, he started a photography business. He was an entrepreneur.

My grandfather was very successful. While most fellow immigrants were working for $1 a day, living in housing owned by the plantation, my grandfather owned a house and a car. It was not long before my grandfather was investing in the stock market and buying beachfront property on Maui, the island where my dad's family lived.

In 1929, the stock market crashed, and the Great Depression began. My grandfather's business dried up, and he soon lost his house, car, and his beachfront property.

My dad was ten years old when the Depression began. That era affected his outlook on life.

He saw Japanese and other immigrants as paid slaves working on the plantations of the rich. He saw his dad, a man who got off the plantation, wiped out by the market crash and economic depression.

In my dad's mind, the only safe way off the plantation was through education. Rather than go to medical school, he chose to become a teacher, with the hope that a good education would provide a way off the plantation for the children of the immigrants. He saw education as an escape from the enslavement by the rich, a passage out of bondage.

My dad dedicated his life to education. He graduated from the University of Hawaii and was soon promoted to principal of a school, the youngest principal at the time. He held a full-time day job and remained in school to obtain higher academic degrees. He was selected for advanced programs at Stanford University, Northwestern University, and the University of Chicago. He worked hard and studied hard as he worked his way up the ladder of public education, eventually becoming the superintendent of education for the State of Hawaii.

My dad would often tell us kids, "The rich brought immigrants to Hawaii to work on their plantations. As soon as the workers arrived, they were put up in plantation housing and were given a charge account at the company store.

"When payday came, the immigrants found the rent for the house and the charges from the company store deducted from their paycheck. At the end of the month, most workers had nothing left. A few owed more money because they charged too much at the company store. Many immigrants never received any money.
They worked for free."

He would end his talk by saying, "This is why you have to study hard—so you can get a job off the plantation."

In my father's immediate family, education was cherished. Most of my relatives have advanced degrees. Many relatives have master's degrees and a few have their doctorate degrees. I am one of the few with only a Bachelor of Science degree.

The problem is that many of my relatives work for the biggest plantation of all, the government. A few of their highly educated children work for modern plantations with names such as Coca-Cola, United Airlines, Bank of America, and IBM.

Most of my family, although highly educated, never made it off the plantation.

Producing Proletariat

Karl Marx defined the proletariat as a class of capitalist society that does not have ownership of the means of production. All they have to sell is their labor for a wage.

This is what our school systems do. Schools produce the proletariat class of a capitalist society. Schools do not teach people to be capitalists.

Today, the working class wants high-paying jobs, but true capitalists are moving the production, hence the jobs, to low-wage countries. This is the real crisis. How can an economy come back if jobs are scarce and wages are low?

Due to a lack of financial education, even the highly educated workers have their wealth siphoned off by debt via the banking system, their retirement via the investment-banking system, their labor via taxes, and what is left via inflation. If they own shares of a company, they own common shares—common shares for common people.

The plantation system is alive and well, even in the Information Age.

The Plantation System

In 2011, kids still go to school, learning nothing about money.

In 2011, kids still come out of school looking for a job, anxious to get married, buy a home, and raise a family.

In 2011, the national debt is out of control, and foreclosures take homes from millions of homeowners.

In 2011, our wealth is being robbed via higher taxes to pay for this debt, debt that goes to the rich.

In 2011, kids who find jobs are only too happy to have taxes taken from their paychecks before they get paid.

In 2011, kids are only too happy to have money deducted from their paychecks with the illusion that they are investing for their retirement.

In 2011, legislation is now being passed making it legal for the government to take a larger percentage of your wealth when you die.

This is the problem of supporting a school system led by E's and S's, training young people to be E's and S's. This is the problem of having political leaders who are E's and S's leading a capitalist system controlled by B's and I's.

This is what happens when E's and S's do not know the difference between assets and liabilities. They spend their lives working to accumulate liabilities, believing they are assets. They go to school to find a job without knowing that a job is not an asset. They work for money, not knowing that money is no longer money. They buy a house, not knowing that a house is not an asset. They save for their retirement, not knowing that stocks and mutual funds are not really assets. When their jobs are shipped overseas, they go back to school to be retrained for a new job.

And they advise their kids to do the same thing.

A Proposal

Before this financial crisis can truly end, the school system must change.

Since the teachers' union maintains a stranglehold on education, it is easier to start a new educational system alongside the old system rather than change the old system.

My proposal is that we start a new school system to teach young people to be capitalists. Parents who want their children to become entrepreneurs rather than employees could choose to send their kids to the school system for capitalists.

For the best and the brightest in this new school system, we create an academy, much like West Point for the Army, Annapolis for the Navy, Air Force Academy for the Air Force, New London for the Coast Guard, and Kings Point for the Merchant Marine. Rather than a military focus, this academy's focus would be on entrepreneurship and would be named the Academy for Entrepreneurs.

Since only entrepreneurs can create real jobs, this academy would help solve the growing problem of unemployment.

To qualify to teach at the new academy, the instructors would have to be real entrepreneurs, trained to teach and willing to teach for free. If they are really entrepreneurs, they would have the time and not need the money.

In this environment of truly free enterprise, whole new industries could be born around innovative technology. Investors would be more willing to risk capital on projects that were intelligently developed.

In this environment of truly free enterprise, many of our most pressing problems, such as global warming, pollution, deforestation, and famine, could be solved. Rather than use government funds to solve problems, entrepreneurs could turn problems into profits, which is what true entrepreneurs do anyway.

Today, we have law schools for lawyers and medical schools for doctors. Why not a school system dedicated to entrepreneurship and capitalism?

Rather than students leaving school looking for a high-paying job, students would leave looking for opportunities to create high-paying jobs. Rather than students leaving school wanting to be paid more for less work, students would leave school seeking opportunities to produce more to earn more. Rather than students leaving school looking for job security or tenure, students would leave school able to create sustainable sources of revenue. Rather than leave school believing the rich are greedy, students would leave school wanting to be the rich who are generous.

An Unfair ROI

Most financial planners, insurance agents, stockbrokers, and some real estate agents will tell you to expect an eight percent to 12 percent ROI (return on investment) per year.

Their sales pitches are made by looking into the past—not gazing into the future.

The years between 2000 and 2010 have been called the "Lost Decade." For millions of amateur stock market investors, their ROI has been less than two percent, for some even zero percent when inflation is factored in.

In real estate, millions lost everything—in some cases, more than everything if they buried themselves in debt trying to save a home that they never really owned anyway. A few professional investors also lost everything.

However, for a few professional investors in both stocks and real estate, the "Lost Decade" has been their "Best Decade."

One unfair advantage of a financial education is the possibility of a much higher ROI on your money, with much less risk, and (in many cases, with the help of a good accountant) zero taxes.

For example, in this book you've seen how the rich, with financial education, earn a minimum of a 28 percent cash-on-cash return in year one, that's guaranteed by the U.S. government.

This means that if you put $100,000 into an investment, you receive $28,000 cash back from the government, cash you can use or invest in whatever you want. Generally, I just reinvest my tax savings.

On top of that, if successful, the investment pays you a dividend every month, income that is taxed at lower rates.

Today, when someone calls me pitching an investment, if the investment he or she is proposing does not guarantee a 28 percent return the first year, cash in my pocket, I turn the investment down. Why risk my money when I can get a government-guaranteed return?

The lowest return I will consider is 28 percent. On many of my investments, even a 100 percent or 250 percent return is not enough. I want an infinite return.

An infinite return means I want all of my investment back.

For example, if I invest $100,000, I want my entire $100,000 returned within three years or less. In addition, I still want to own the asset, plus I want cash-flow income every month, and I want my income and the return of my $100,000—tax free.

The dollar amount is not significant. The investment can be $10,000 or $10 million. The difference depends upon your financial education.

In simple terms, an infinite return is your way of printing your own money. Every month you receive a check for nothing, free money, just like the Federal Reserve Bank.

The rock band Dire Straits had a hit song years ago, "Money for nothing, chicks for free." I can't guarantee free chicks, but I can guarantee money for nothing for myself. If you have a solid financial education and invest with smart, legal, and ethical people, people who also have a solid financial education, you too can earn money for nothing.

Money for nothing is your real ROI for your investment in your financial education. While there are never guarantees in the world of money, a legitimate financial education grants you access to the highest returns in the investment world, investments with the lowest risks, and very low taxes, zero taxes in some instances. The first investment is in your financial education.

It's Too Good to Be True

You can be sure that most financial planners, stockbrokers, real estate agents, and insurance agents will say, "If it seems too good to be true, it's probably not true."

People who sell investments feel they have to downplay or discourage investments claiming to do better than the investments they sell, labeling them as "risky."

And it is too good to be true for most people—people without financial education.

Investing for Dummies

I have always found it amusing that people think saving money is smart. Or that turning your money over to a financial planner who invests your money in mutual funds is smart.

It takes zero intelligence to save money. It takes zero financial education or financial intelligence to turn your money over to a financial planner.

An animal trainer can train a monkey to save money and invest in mutual funds. It's simple: The monkey drops off its money at the bank, and the animal trainer gives the monkey a banana. Smart monkey. It's even easier to train a monkey to invest in mutual funds. All the monkey has to do is have his investment withdrawn from his paycheck along with taxes and retirement money, money the monkey will never see.

You may notice that the only difference between the word monkey and money is the letter "k" which stands for "knowledge," or in the case of the monkey, the *lack of knowledge*. Without knowledge, there is not much difference between a monkey with money and a monkey without money.

Today there are a lot of humans without money, yet they still deposit what they earn in the bank and have their retirement funds withdrawn from their paycheck before they get their paycheck.

I repeat: It takes no financial education to save money. Today, saving money is actually stupid, especially in an environment where the central banks are printing trillions of dollars. Saving money is like investing in "original Picassos" as they come off the printing press. We're talking reproduction… not real.

The best way to beat the central banks is to print your own *real money*. I have been printing my own *real money* for years—legally, ethically, and morally, and with the blessing of the government.

You can do the same, but first you must invest in your financial education—because your financial education is your unfair advantage to gaining an infinite ROI.

In closing, my rich dad often said, "Your brain is your greatest asset. Your brain can also be your greatest liability."

I wrote this book to give you the unfair advantage of turning your brain into your greatest asset.

If you fail to turn your brain into an asset, don't worry. You can always be a monkey. As you know, monkeys do not know the difference between bananas and real money. To them, it's all the same.

Afterword

"I hated school – but I love learning."

The Purpose of Education

The true purpose of education is to grant a person the power to turn information into meaning. The trouble in the Information Age is that there is an avalanche of financial information and a lack of financial education.

Without financial education, millions of people are no better than a Pavlovian dog, doing as they are trained to do. Ring the school bell, and employees find a job and turn their money over to the government, bankers, and Wall Street.

What Do I Do?

A few days ago, I went into my local health-food store. The clerk who works in the store is a wealth of knowledge. He has a master's degree in agriculture and worked as a farmer. Unfortunately, a three-year drought and back taxes cost him his family farm. He found a job working in a health-food store specializing in organic produce. He has been a hardworking employee, managing the store for over twenty years.

As he was ringing up my purchases, he said, "Did you know the Federal Reserve Bank is not federal?"

"Yes," I said, nodding my head.

"Do you know the Fed and the U.S. Treasury are printing trillions of dollars out of thin air?"

Again I nodded my head.

"Have you noticed the price of food going up—even though the government says there is no inflation?"

"Yes," I said. "I have noticed the prices creeping up."

"So how can the government say there is no inflation?"

"I've wondered that myself."

Placing the food in the bags, he asked, "May I ask you a question?"

"Sure."

"Are we in trouble?"

"Some people are," I said.

"I don't have anything," he said. "I have a few dollars in savings. I've been a renter all my life because my credit rating is so bad. And my retirement plan was destroyed by the crash, so I pulled my money out early and was penalized for early withdrawal."

I just shook my head silently.

"What can I do? Is it too late for me to start over? Am I too old?"

"How old are you?" I asked.

"I'm 52."

"You have a lot of time," I said. "Colonel Sanders started Kentucky Fried Chicken when he was 66."

"He had to start over at 66?"

"Yes. He went broke when a new highway bypassed his single-store fried-chicken business. Once he saw how much his Social Security check was, he knew he was in trouble. So he packed his bags and began selling the rights to his special recipe to restaurants across the United States. He was turned down over 1,000 times before someone finally said yes. That led to his franchise operation. He took it public on the stock exchange, and he became a rich and famous man. Today, you can find Kentucky Fried Chicken all over the world. He has made a lot of people rich."

"Organic food is a growing business. Do you think I could do the same thing?"

"You might."

"Should I go back to school?"

"Education is important," I said. "But you might want to look for a different type of school."

The Times They Are A-Changin'

There have been many changes in our economy and the investing landscape since *Rich Dad Poor Dad* was first published in 1997. Fourteen years ago, Robert Kiyosaki challenged conventional wisdom with his bold statement that, "Your house is not an asset." His contrarian views on money and investing were met with outrage and criticism.

In 2002, *Rich Dad's Prophecy* advised that we prepare for an upcoming financial market crash. In 2006, Robert joined forces with Donald Trump to write *Why We Want You To Be Rich,* a book that was inspired by their concern for the shrinking middle class in America.

Robert continues to be a passionate advocate for the importance and power of financial education. Today, in the wake of the subprime fiasco, record home foreclosures, and a global economic meltdown that is still raging, his words seem not only prophetic, but enlightened. Many skeptics have become believers.

In preparing the 2011 reprint of *Rich Dad's CASHFLOW Quadrant* book, Robert realized two things: that his message and teachings have withstood the test of time, and that the investment landscape, the world in which investors operate, has changed dramatically. These changes have affected, and will continue to affect, those in the I (Investor) quadrant and have fueled Robert's decision to update an important section in the *CASHFLOW Quadrant* book which specifically addresses investors.

The following special section in *Unfair Advantage* is a gift from Robert, a sneak preview of the new chapter from *Rich Dad's CASHFLOW Quadrant:* "Five Levels of Investors."

FIVE LEVELS
OF INVESTORS

My poor dad often said, "Investing is risky."

My rich dad often said, "Being financially uneducated is risky."

Today, most people know they should invest. The problem is that most people, like my poor dad, believe investing is risky—and investing is risky if you lack financial education, experience, and guidance.

Learning to invest is important because investing is the key to financial freedom. Five things happen to people who do not invest, or who invest poorly:

1. They work hard all their lives.
2. They worry about money all their lives.
3. They depend on others, such as family, a company pension, or the government, to take care of them.
4. The boundaries of their lives are defined by money.
5. They will not know what true freedom is.

Rich dad often said, "You will never know true freedom until you achieve financial freedom." By this, he meant that learning to invest is more important than learning a profession. He said, "When you learn a profession, let's say to be a doctor, you learn how to work for money. Learning to invest is learning how to have money work for you. The moment you have money working for you, you have your ticket to freedom." He also said, "The more money you have working for you, the less you pay in taxes—if you are a true investor."

Learning to Invest

My rich dad began preparing me for the I quadrant at the age of nine using the game of *Monopoly®* as a teaching tool. Over and over again, he would say, "One of the great formulas for wealth is found in the game of *Monopoly*. Always remember the formula: four green houses, one red hotel."

The game of *Monopoly* is a game of cash flow. For example, if you had one green house on a property you owned and you received $10, that was $10 a month in cash flow. Two houses, $20. Three houses, $30. And the red hotel, $50. More green houses and more red hotels mean more cash flow, less work, less taxes, and more freedom.

A simple game, but an important lesson.

Rich dad played *Monopoly* in real life. He would often take his son and me to visit his green houses—green houses that would one day become a big red hotel, right on Waikiki Beach.

As I grew up and watched my rich dad play the game of *Monopoly* in real life, I learned many valuable lessons about investing. Some of those lessons are:

- Investing is not risky.
- Investing is fun.
- Investing can make you very, very, rich.
- More importantly, investing can set you free, free from the struggle of earning a living and worrying about money.

In other words, if you were smart, you could build a pipeline of cash flow for life, a pipeline that would produce cash in good times and bad, in market booms and market crashes. Your cash flow would increase automatically with inflation and, at the same time, allow you to pay less in taxes.

I am not saying real estate is the only way to invest. I use the game of *Monopoly* simply as an example of how the rich get richer. A person can earn income from stocks via dividends, from bonds via interest, or from oil, books, and patents via royalties.

In other words, there are many ways to financial freedom.

Financial "Experts"

Unfortunately, due to a lack of financial education in schools, most people blindly turn their money over to people they believe are financial experts: people such as bankers, financial planners, and stockbrokers. Unfortunately, most of these "experts" are not really investors in the I quadrant. Most are employees in the E quadrant working for a paycheck, or they are self-employed financial advisors in the S quadrant working for fees and commissions. Most "experts" cannot afford to stop working, simply because they don't have investments working for them.

Warren Buffett said, "Wall Street is the only place where people ride to work in a Rolls Royce to get advice from those who take the subway."

If people do not have sound financial education, they cannot tell if a financial advisor is a salesman or a con man, a fool or a genius. Remember, all con men are nice people. If they were not being nice by telling you what you want to hear, you would not listen to them.

There is nothing wrong with being a sales person. We all have something to sell. Yet, as Warren Buffet says, "Never ask an insurance salesman if you need insurance." When it comes to money, there are many people desperate enough to tell and sell you anything, just to get your money.

Interestingly, the vast majority of investors never meet the person taking their money. In most of the Western world, employees simply have their money automatically deducted from their paycheck, in the same way the tax department collects taxes. Many workers in America simply allow their employer to deduct their money and put it into their 401(k) retirement plan, possibly the worst way to invest for retirement. (401(k) plans go by different names in different countries. In Australia they are called superannuation plans, in Japan they are also called 401(k)s, and in Canada they are known as RRSPs.)

I say the 401(k) may possibly be the worst way to invest for retirement for the following reasons:

> **1. TIME magazine is on my side.** *TIME* magazine has run a number of articles over the years, questioning the wisdom of putting so many people's retirement at risk. *TIME* has been

predicting that millions will not have enough money to retire after a lifetime of turning their money over to strangers.

A typical 401(k) plan takes 80 percent of the profits. The investor may receive 20 percent of the profits, if they are lucky. The investor puts up 100 percent of the money and takes 100 percent of the risk. The 401(k) plan puts up 0 percent of the money and takes 0 percent of the risk. The fund makes money, even if you lose money.

2. Taxes work against you with a 401(k). Long-term capital gains are taxed at a lower rate of around 15%. But the 401(k) treats any gains as ordinary earned income. Ordinary income is taxed at the highest rate, sometimes as high as 35%. And if you want to take the money out early, you'll have to pay an additional 10% penalty tax.

3. You have no insurance if there is a stock-market crash. To drive a car, I must have insurance in case there is a crash. When I invest in real estate, I have insurance in case of fire or other losses. Yet the 401(k) investor has no insurance to prevent losses from market crashes.

4. The 401(k) is for people who are planning to be poor when they retire. That is why financial planners often say, "When you retire, you'll be taxed at a lower tax rate." They assume your income will go down in retirement into a lower tax bracket. If, on the other hand, you are rich when you retire and you have a 401(k), you could pay even higher taxes at retirement. Smart investors understand taxes before investing.

5. Income from a 401(k) is withdrawn at ordinary earned income-tax rates, the highest of the three types of income, which are:

1. Ordinary earned
2. Portfolio
3. Passive

The sad truth about most financial advisors and pension-fund managers is that they are not investors. Most are employees in the E quadrant. One reason why so many government pensions and union pensions are in trouble is because these employees are not trained to be investors. Most do not have any real-life financial education.

To make matters worse, most financial "experts" advise uneducated investors to "invest for the long term in a well-diversified portfolio of stocks, bonds, and mutual funds."

Why do these financial "experts," employees in the E quadrant or sales people in the S quadrant masquerading as investors in the I quadrant, advise you to do that? It's because they get paid, not by how much money they make for you, but by how much money you turn over to them for the long term. The longer your money is parked with them, the more they get paid.

The reality is that real investors do not park their money. They move their money. It is a strategy known as the "velocity of money." A true investor's money is always moving, acquiring new assets, and then moving on to acquire even more assets. Only amateurs park their money.

I am not saying that 401(k)-type plans are bad, although I would never have one. For me, they are too expensive, too risky, too tax-inefficient, and not fair to the investor.

I am saying there are better ways to invest, but they require financial education.

What Is the Best Investment?

The average investor does not know the difference between investing for cash flow and investing for capital gains. Most investors invest for capital gains, hoping and praying the price of their stock or home goes up. As long as you have more cash flowing in than flowing out, your investment is a good investment.

Keep in mind that it's not the asset class that makes a person rich or poor. For example, when a person asks, "Is real estate is a good investment?" I reply, "I don't know. Are you a good investor?" Or if they ask, "Are stocks a good investment?" again my answer is the same, "I don't know. Are you a good investor?"

My point is that it is never the investment or asset class that is important. Success or failure, wealth or poverty, depends solely on how smart the investor is. A smart investor will make millions in the stock market. An amateur will lose millions.

Tragically, most people do not think learning to invest is important. This is why most people believe investing is risky and turn their money over to "experts," most of whom are not really investors, but sales people who make money whether the investor makes money or loses money.

There are five types or levels of investors found in the I quadrant.

Five Different Levels of Investors

Level 1: The Zero-Financial-Intelligence Level

Sadly, in America, once the richest country in the world, over 50 percent of the U.S. population is at the bottom level of the I quadrant. Simply said, they have nothing to invest.

There are many people who make a lot of money who fall into this category. They earn a lot—and spend more than they earn.

I have a friend who looks very rich. He has a good job as a real estate broker, a beautiful wife, and three kids in private school. They live in a beautiful house overlooking the Pacific Ocean in San Diego. He and his wife drive expensive European cars. When his son and daughters were old enough, they too drove expensive cars. They looked rich, but what they had was debt. They looked rich, but were poorer than most poor people.

Now, they are homeless. When the real estate market crashed, they crashed. They were no longer able to pay the interest on all the debt they had accumulated.

When we were younger, this same friend made a lot of money. Unfortunately, it was his low financial-intelligence level—zero—that caused him be a zero over the long run. In fact, he is so deeply in debt that he is really a sub-zero investor.

Like many people, everything he buys loses value or costs him money. Nothing he buys makes him richer.

Level 2: The Savers-Are-Losers Level

Many people believe it is smart to save money. The problem is that today, money is no longer money. Today, people are saving counterfeit dollars, money that can be created at the speed of light.

In 1971 President Nixon took the U.S. dollar off the gold standard, and money became debt. The primary reason why prices have risen since 1971 is simply because the United States now has the power to print money to pay its bills.

Today, savers are the biggest losers. Since 1971, the U.S. dollar has lost 95 percent of its value when compared to gold. It will not take another 40 years to lose its remaining 5 percent.

Remember, in 1971, gold was $35 an ounce. Forty years later, gold is over $1,400 an ounce. That is a massive loss of purchasing power for the dollar. The problem grows worse as the U.S. national debt escalates into the trillions of dollars, and the U.S. continues to print more counterfeit money.

As the Federal Reserve Bank and central banks throughout the world print trillions of dollars at high speed, every printed dollar means higher taxes and more inflation. In spite of this fact, millions of people continue to believe that saving money is smart. It used to be smart when money was money.

The biggest market in the world is the bond market. "Bond" is another word for "savings." There are many different types of bonds for the different types of savers. There are U.S. Treasury bonds, corporate bonds, municipal bonds, and junk bonds.

For years, it was assumed that U.S. government bonds and government municipal bonds were safe. Then the financial crisis of 2007 began. As many of you know, the crisis was caused by mortgage bonds, such as mortgage-backed securities or MBS, also known as derivatives. Millions of these mortgage bonds were made up of subprime mortgages, which were loans to subprime or high-risk borrowers. You may recall that some of those borrowers had no income and no job. Yet, they were buying homes they could never pay for.

The Wall Street bankers took these subprime loans and packaged them into bonds, magically got this subprime bond labeled as prime, and sold them to institutions, banks, governments, and individual investors. To me, this is fraud. But that is the banking system.

Once the subprime borrower could no longer pay the interest on their mortgages, these MBS bonds began blowing up all over the world.

Interestingly, it was Warren Buffett's firm, Moody's, that blessed these subprime mortgages as AAA prime debt, the highest rating for bonds.

Today, many people blame the big banks such as Goldman Sachs and J. P. Morgan for the crisis. Yet, if anyone should be blamed for this crisis, it should be Warren Buffet. He is a smart man, and he knew what he was doing. Moody's was blessing rotting dog meat as Grade A prime beef. That is criminal.

The problem is that these subprime bonds are now causing ripple effects all over the world. Today, countries such as Ireland and Greece are in serious trouble, unable to pay the interest on their bonds. In the United States, governments and municipalities are going broke, unable to pay the interest on their bonds.

In 2011, millions of individuals, many retirees, pension funds, governments, and banks are in trouble as the bond market proves how unsafe bonds can be.

On top of that, rising inflation makes bonds an even riskier investment, which is why savers who only know how to save are losers. For example, if a bond is paying 3 percent interest and inflation is running at 5 percent, the value of a 3 percent bond crashes, wiping out the investors' value.

China could be the biggest loser of all. China holds a trillion dollars in U.S. bonds. Every time the U.S. government devalues the dollar by printing more money and issuing more bonds, the value of China's trillion-dollar investment in the United States goes down. If China stops buying U.S. government bonds, the world economy will stop and crash.

Millions of retirees are just like China. Retirees in need of a steady income after retirement believed government bonds were safe. Today, as governments, big and small, go bust and inflation rises, retirees are finding out that savers who saved money in bonds are losers.

Municipal bonds are IOUs issued by states, cities, hospitals, schools, and other public institutions. One advantage of municipal bonds is that many are tax-free income. The problem is that municipal bonds are not risk-free.

Millions of municipal-bond investors are now finding out that the municipal bonds they invested in are in serious trouble. In the United States, more than $3 trillion are invested in municipal bonds. It is estimated that two thirds of those bonds are now at risk because these public institutions are broke. If more money is not pumped in, the United States could implode from the center as states, cities, hospitals, and schools begin to default, just as subprime homeowners defaulted and stopped paying on their home mortgages.

The bond market is the biggest market in the world, bigger than the stock market or the real estate market. The main reason it is the biggest is because most people are savers, Level 2 investors. Unfortunately, after 1971 when the rules of money changed, savers became the biggest losers, even if they saved money by investing in bonds.

Remember that savers, bondholders, and most people who save money in a retirement plan, are people who park their money, investing for the long term, while professional investors move their money. Professional investors invest their money in an asset, get their money back without selling the asset, and move their money on to buy more assets. This is why savers, who park their money, are the biggest losers.

Level 3: The I'm-Too-Busy Level

This is the investor who is too busy to learn about investing. Many investors at this level are highly educated people who are simply too busy with their careers, family, other interests, and vacations. Hence, they prefer to remain financially naïve and turn their money over to someone else to manage for them.

This is the level that most 401(k)s, IRAs, and even very rich investors are at. They simply turn their money over to an "expert," and then hope and pray their expert is really an expert.

Soon after the financial crisis broke in 2007, many affluent people found out their trusted expert was not an expert at all and, even worse, could not be trusted.

In a matter of months, trillions of dollars of wealth vaporized as real estate and stock markets began to crash. Panicking, these investors called their trusted advisors and begged for salvation.

A few rich investors found out that their trusted advisors were extremely sophisticated con men, running elaborate Ponzi schemes. A Ponzi scheme is an investment scheme where investors are paid off with new investors' money. The scheme works as long as there are new investors adding new money to pay off the old investors. In the United States, Bernie Madoff became famous because he "made off" with billions in rich people's money.

There are legal Ponzi schemes and illegal Ponzi schemes. Social Security is a legal Ponzi scheme, as is the stock market. In both instances, the scheme works as long as new money flows into the scheme. If new money stops flowing in, the scheme—be it Madoff's scheme, Social Security, or Wall Street—collapses.

The problem with the Level-3 investor, the I'm-too-busy investor, is that the person learns nothing if they lose their money. They have no experience except a bad experience. All they can do is blame their advisor, the market, or the government. It's hard to learn from one's mistakes if the person does not know what mistakes were made.

Level 4: The I'm-a-Professional Level

This is the do-it-yourselfer investor. When you look at the CASHFLOW Quadrant, they are in the S quadrant as an investor.

Many retirees become Level-4 investors once their working days are over.

This investor may buy and sell a few stocks, often from a discount broker. After all, why should they pay a stockbroker's higher commissions when they do their own research and make their own decisions?

If they invest in real estate, the do-it-yourselfer will find, fix, and manage their own properties.

And if the person is a gold bug, they will buy and store their own gold and silver.

In most cases, the do-it-yourselfer has very little, if any, formal financial education. After all, if they can do it themselves, why should they learn anything?

If they do attend a course or two, it is often in a narrow subject area. For example, if they like stock trading, they will focus only on stock trading. The same is true for the small real estate investor.

At the age of nine, when rich dad began my financial education with the game of *Monopoly*, he wanted me to have a bigger picture of the world of investing. The following are some of the basic big-picture asset classes he wanted me to spend my life learning. They are:

BALANCE SHEET

Assets	Liabilities
Business	
Real Estate	
Paper Assets	
Commodities	

As more people realize the need to invest, millions of them will become small Level-4 investors in all four categories.

After the 2007 market crash, millions of people have become entrepreneurs, starting small businesses, and many are investing in real estate while prices are low. Most, however, are trying their hand at stock trading and stock picking. As the dollar declines in value, millions of people are beginning to save gold and silver instead of dollars.

Obviously, those who also invest in their ongoing financial education, taking classes regularly and hiring a coach to enhance their performance, will outpace those who just do it on their own.

With a sound financial education, a few of the Level-4 investors will climb to the next level, the Level-5 investor, the capitalist.

Level 5: The Capitalist Level

This is the richest-people-in-the-world level.

The Level-5 investor, a capitalist, is skilled as a business owner from the B quadrant investing in the I quadrant.

As stated earlier, the Level-4 investor is the do-it-yourselfer from the S quadrant investing in the I quadrant.

The following are a few examples of the differences between a Level-4 investor and a Level-5 capitalist investor.

1. The S-quadrant investor generally uses his or her own money to invest.

   The B-quadrant investor generally uses OPM (other people's money) to invest.

   This is one of the major differences between the Level-4 and Level-5 investor.

2. The S-quadrant investor is often a solo investor. (S also stands for smartest.)

   The B-quadrant investor invests with a team. B-quadrant investors do not have to be the smartest. They just have to have the smartest team.

   Most people know that two minds are better than one. Yet, many S-quadrant investors believe they are the smartest people in the world.

3. The S-quadrant investor earns less than the B-quadrant investor.

4. The S-quadrant investor often pays higher taxes than the B-quadrant investor.

5. The S quadrant also stands for selfish. The more selfish they are, the more money they make.

   The B-quadrant investor must be generous. The more generous they are, the more money they make.

6. It is difficult to raise money as an S-quadrant investor.

It is easy for a B-quadrant investor to raise capital. Once a person knows how to build a business in the B quadrant, success attracts money. It becomes easy to raise money in the I quadrant if you are successful in the B quadrant. That is the big "if."

The ease of raising capital is one of the biggest differences between being successful in the S quadrant versus being successful in the B quadrant. Once a person is successful in the B quadrant, life is easy. The challenge is becoming successful.

The problem with success in the S quadrant is that raising capital is always difficult.

For example, it is easy to take a B-quadrant business public via selling shares of the business on the stock market. The story of Facebook is a modern example of how easy it is to raise capital for a B-quadrant business. If Facebook had remained just a small web-consulting firm, it would have been very difficult to raise investor capital.

Another example is McDonald's. If McDonald's had remained just a single hamburger store, an S-quadrant operation, no one would have invested in it. Once McDonald's began expanding into the B quadrant via a franchise system and was listed on the stock exchange, money poured in.

The reason a business sells "shares" is because the more they share, the richer the entrepreneur becomes. An S-quadrant business has a tough time selling shares because the business is too small to share.

In real estate, the same is true. When I was a small real estate investor investing in single-family homes, condos, and small 4- to 30-unit apartment buildings, it was difficult getting loans. The moment Kim and I began investing in apartment buildings with over 100 units, banks were more willing to lend us much more money. The reason: On 100-unit-plus properties priced in the millions, banks do not finance the investor. They finance the investment. In other words, on properties of over 100 units, banks look more closely at the investment than the investor.

On top of that, bankers would rather lend $10 million than $10,000 since it takes just as much time to lend thousands as it does millions. Remember, bankers love debtors because debtors make the bank rich.

Once bankers are satisfied with our ability to own and manage large apartment houses profitably, banks often line up to offer us money, even during a crisis.

So the question is: Who do Level-5 investors get their money from? The answer is: They get their money from Level-2 and Level-3 investors who save their money in banks and pension plans.

Starting with Nothing

The reason I started this book with the story of Kim and me being homeless is to let readers know that not having any money is not an excuse for not growing smarter, thinking bigger, and becoming richer.

For most of my life, I have never had enough money. If I had let not having money be an excuse, I would never have become a capitalist. This is important, because a true capitalist never has money. That is why they must know how to raise capital and use other people's money to make a lot of money for a lot of people.

How to Become a Capitalist

My mom and dad wanted me to be successful in the E and S quadrants. My dad suggested I go to school, get my PhD, which he did himself, and work for the government or climb a corporate ladder in the E quadrant. My mom, a registered nurse, wanted me to become a medical doctor in the S quadrant.

My rich dad suggested I become a capitalist. That meant I had to study the skills required for success in the B and I quadrants.

My mom and dad believed in traditional schools such as colleges, law schools, and medical schools. They valued good grades, degrees, and credentials, such as a law degree or a medical license.

My rich dad believed in education, but not the type of education found in traditional schools. Rather than go to school, my rich dad signed up for seminars and courses that improved his business and investing skills. He also took personal-development courses. He was not interested in grades or credentials. He wanted real-life skills that gave him strengths and operational skills in the B and I quadrants.

When I was in high school, my rich dad often flew to Honolulu to attend seminars on entrepreneurship and investing. One day, when I told my poor dad that rich dad was going to a class on sales, my poor dad laughed. He could not understand why anyone would want to learn how to sell, especially if the class hours were not applied as credit to an advanced college degree. My poor dad also looked down upon my rich dad because my rich dad never finished high school.

Having two dads with differing attitudes on education, I was aware that there was more than one type of education. Traditional schools were for those who wanted to be successful in the E and S quadrants, and another type of education was for those who wanted to be successful in the B and I quadrants.

In 1973, I returned from Vietnam. It was time for me to make up my mind about which dad I was going to follow. Was I going to follow in my poor dad's footsteps and go back to school to become an E or an S, or take my rich dad's path and become a B or an I, eventually to become a capitalist?

In 1973, my rich dad suggested I take classes on real estate investing. He said, "If you want to be a successful capitalist, you must know how to raise capital and how to use debt to make money."

That year I took a three-day workshop on real estate investing. It was the start of my education into the world of the capitalist.

A few months later, after looking at over 100 properties, I purchased my first rental property on the island of Maui, using 100 percent debt financing and still putting $25 cash flow in my pocket each month. My real-life education had begun. I was learning to use other people's money to make money, a skill a true capitalist must know.

In 1974, my contract with the Marine Corps was up, and I took a job with the Xerox Corporation in Hawaii, not because I wanted to climb the corporate ladder, but because Xerox had the best sales-training program. Again, this was all part of my rich dad's educational program to train me to become a capitalist.

By 1994, Kim and I were financially free, never needing a job or a company or government retirement plan. Rich dad was correct: My education could set me free—but not the education found in traditional schools.

When the markets began to crash in 2007, rather than crash with the rest of the economy, our wealth skyrocketed. As the stock market and real estate markets crashed, great deals floated to the surface, and banks were more than eager to lend us millions of dollars to buy and take over their investments gone bad. In 2010 alone, Kim and I acquired over $87 million in real estate, using loans from banks and pension funds. That year was our best year so far.

As rich dad often said, "If you are a true investor, it does not matter if the markets are going up or coming down. A true investor does well in any market condition."

Where Are You?

Take a moment and assess where you are today.

Are You at Investor Level 1?

If there is nothing in your asset column with no income coming in from your investments and you have too many liabilities, then you are starting at the bottom level, ground zero.

If you are deeply in bad debt, your best investment might be to get out of bad debt.

There is nothing wrong with being deeply in bad debt, unless you do nothing. After I lost my first business, I was nearly a million dollars in debt. It took me almost five years to reach zero. In many ways, learning from my mistakes and taking responsibility for my mistakes was the best education I could have asked for. If I had not learned from my mistakes, I would not be where I am today.

Kim and I put together a simple program and workbook explaining the process we used to get out of hundreds of thousands of dollars of bad debt. It is a simple, almost painless, process. All it takes is a little discipline and a willingness to learn.

The title of the product is *"How We Got Out of Bad Debt."* You can purchase it online from RichDad.com

Are You at Investor Level 2?

If you are a saver, be very careful, especially if you are saving money in a bank or in a retirement plan. In general, savers are losers.

Saving is often a strategy for people who do not want to learn anything. You see, it takes no financial intelligence to save. You can train a monkey to save money.

The risk in saving is that you learn little. And if your savings are wiped out, either by market decline or devaluation of the money supply, you wind up without money and without education.

Remember that the U.S. dollar has lost 95 percent of its value since 1971. It will not take long to lose the rest of its value.

As stated, a person can even lose money saving gold if they buy gold at the wrong price.

I suggest taking a few courses on investing, either in stocks or real estate, and see if anything interests you.

If nothing interests you, then keep saving.

Remember that the bond market is the biggest market in the world simply because most people and businesses are savers, not investors. This may sound strange to savers, but the bond market and banks need borrowers.

Are You at Investor Level 3?

This level is similar to Level 2, except that this level invests in riskier instruments, such as stocks, bonds, mutual funds, insurance, and exchange-traded funds.

Again, the risk with this level is that, if everything is lost, the investor loses everything—and learns nothing.

If you are ready to move out of Level 3, invest in your financial education and take control of your money, then Level 4 is a good level for you.

Are You at Investor Level 4?

If you are here as a professional investor, congratulations. Very few people invest the time to learn and manage their own money. The key to success at Level 4 is lifelong learning, great teachers, great coaches, and like-minded friends.

Level-4 investors take control of their lives, knowing that their mistakes are their opportunities to learn and to grow.

The fear of investing does not frighten them. It challenges them.

Are You at Investor Level 5?

To me, being a capitalist investor at level 5 is like being at the top of the world. Literally, the world is your oyster. The world has no borders. In this world of high-speed technology, it is easier than ever to be a capitalist in a world of plenty.

If you are at this level, keep learning and keep giving. Remember that true capitalists are generous because a B-quadrant capitalist knows you must give more to receive more.

It's Your Choice

One great thing about freedom is the freedom to choose to live the life you want to live.

In 1973 at the age of 26, I knew I did not want to live my life the way my parents chose to live. I did not want to be living below our means, living paycheck to paycheck, trying to make ends meet. For me, this was not living. It may have been good for them, but I knew in my heart that it was not right for me.

I also knew that going back to school for advanced degrees was not for me. I knew school did not make people rich because I grew up in a family of advanced degrees. Most of my uncles and aunts had masters' degrees and a few had their doctorates.

I did not want to climb a corporate ladder in the E quadrant either, nor did I want to be a very special specialist in the S quadrant.

So I took the path less traveled and decided to become an

entrepreneur and professional investor. I wanted the freedom to travel the world, do business, and invest.

It was my choice. I do not recommend that path to everyone. But I do recommend that a person choose. That is what freedom is: the power to choose.

I encourage you to look at the five levels of investors and make your choice. Each level has its pros and cons, its advantages and disadvantages. Each level has a price greater than money.

If you choose Level 1, 2, or 3, there are many other people and organizations qualified to support your investment life at those levels.

In 1997, Kim and I created The Rich Dad Company to provide educational games, programs, and coaches for those individuals who seek to be Level-4 and Level-5 investors.

A Final Word on Investing

In the world of money, you'll often see the term ROI, Return On Investment. Depending upon whom you talk to, ROI will vary. For example, if you talk to a banker, he or she may say, "We pay 3 percent interest on your money." For many people, this may sound good. If you talk to a financial planner, they may say, "You can expect a return on your investment of 10 percent per year." To many people, a 10 percent return is exciting.

To most people, especially those on the E and S side of the quadrant, the higher your return, the greater the risk. So the person accepting a 10 percent return already assumes there is more risk in that investment than the 3 percent return from the bank. And there is.

Ironically, both the 3 percent return from the bank and the 10 percent return from the stock market are extremely high-risk. The money in the bank is at risk due to inflation and higher taxes caused by banks printing money. The 10 percent in the stock market is at risk due to volatility caused by HFT (high-frequency trading) and due to the novice investor investing without insurance.

In my world, ROI stands for a Return On Information. This means that the more information I have, the higher my returns—and the lower my risk.

I caution you, because what I am about to say may sound insane or too good to be true. Yet I assure you, it is true.

In my world, the world of a Level-4 and Level-5 investor, an infinite return is expected—and with low risk. An infinite return means: Money for nothing. In other words, the investor receives income without having any of their own money in the investment.

In an earlier section, I wrote that I took a real estate course in 1973. After looking at over 100 investments, I purchased a condo on Maui using 100 percent financing, which means I used none of my own money. I put $25 each month into my pocket. That $25 was an infinite return on my investment, since I had zero invested. And I quote from that section: "My real-life education had begun. I was learning to use other people's money to make money, a skill a true capitalist must know."

I know $25 a month is not a lot of money. Yet, it was not the money that was important to me. It was learning a new way of thinking, a way of processing information and producing a result.

One of the reasons that I have so much money today is simply because I was educated and trained to think differently. If you have read *Rich Dad Poor Dad*, you may recall that the title for chapter one of the book is, "The Rich Don't Work For Money." One of the reasons why those in the E and S quadrants have problems with that statement is because most went to school to learn to work for money. They did not go to school to learn how to have other people's money work for them.

When Kim and I started The Rich Dad Company, we borrowed $250,000 from investors. We paid the money back once the company was up and running. Today, the business has returned multi-millions of dollars, not only to Kim and me, but to companies and individuals associated with Rich Dad. As I said, capitalists are generous.

My point is that, the moment a person knows how to make money out of nothing or with other people's money or a bank's money, they enter a different world. It's a world almost exactly opposite the world of those in the E and S quadrants where they experience hard work, high taxes, and low returns on investment.

The reason most people believe saving is smart and a 10 percent return in the stock market is worth it is simply due to a lack of financial education.

Your best ROI is not a return on your investment, but a return on your information. This is why a financial education is essential, especially for the uncertainty of the world ahead.

Remember this about the word "education": Education gives us the power to turn information into meaning. In the Information Age, we are drenched with financial information. Yet, without financial education, we cannot turn information into useful meaning for our lives.

In closing, I say the I quadrant is the most important quadrant for your future. No matter what you do for a living, how well you do in the I quadrant will determine your future. In other words, even if you make very little money in the E or S quadrant, financial education in the I quadrant is your ticket to freedom and financial security.

For example, my sister is a Buddhist nun. She earns nearly zero in the S quadrant. Yet she attends our investment courses and has steadily been increasing her financial education. Today, her future is bright because she got out of saving money in the bank and buying mutual funds and began investing in real estate and silver. In the ten years between 2000 and 2010, she has made much more money in the I quadrant than she could ever make as a nun in the S quadrant.

I am very proud of my sister. She may be a nun by profession, but she does not have to be a poor nun.

Before Reading Further

This completes the explanation part of the CASHFLOW Quadrant. Before we go on, here's the big question:

1. What level of investor are you?

   _____

If you're truly sincere about getting wealthy quickly, read and reread the five levels. Each time I read the levels, I see a little of myself in all the levels. I recognize not only strengths, but also character flaws that hold me back. The way to great financial wealth is to strengthen your strengths and address your character flaws. And the way to do that is by first recognizing them rather than pretending that you're perfect.

We all want to think the best of ourselves. I've dreamed of being a Level-5 capitalist for most of my life. I knew this was what I wanted to become from the moment my rich dad explained the similarities between a stock picker and a person who bets on horses. But after studying the different levels of this list, I could see the character flaws that held me back. I found character flaws in myself from Level 4 that would often rear their ugly heads in times of pressure. The gambler in me was good, but it was also not so good. So with the guidance of Kim, my friends and additional schooling, I began addressing my own character flaws and turning them into strengths. My effectiveness as a Level-5 investor improved immediately.

Although I do operate today as a Level-5 investor, I continue to read and reread the five levels and work on improving myself.

Here's another question for you:
2. What level of investor do you want or need to be in the near future?

_____

If your answer to question two is the same as that in question one, then you are where you want to be. If you are happy where you are, relative to being an investor, then there's not much need to read any further in this book. One of life's greatest joys is to be happy where you are. Congratulations!

Warning
Anyone with the goal of becoming a Level-5 Investor must develop their skills FIRST as a Level-4 investor. Level 4 can't be skipped on your path to Level 5. Anyone who tries to do this is really a Level-3 investor—a gambler!

Bonus

FAQs

SECTIONS 1 THROUGH 8

As a bonus...

I have added a special section on FAQs—eight of them—about Rich Dad's financial education and programs.

With every FAQ answer, I will include why I believe the programs we offer are important and essential for success in the brave new world of the new economy and how they can benefit you as you invest in yourself. You can choose to be a part of the solution in addressing the challenges we face in our world.

Robert Kiyosaki

Bonus FAQ #1: What Is the Rich Dad Difference?

FAQ
What makes Rich Dad's financial education programs different?

Short Answer
We start by making financial education fun, entertaining, and simple. Then you can decide where you want to go and how far you want to go.

Explanation
Most financial education programs start with the small picture. Ads you see on TV, on the web, or in print are often about investing techniques: techniques such as stock trading, or foreign-exchange currency trading, or flip this house, or real estate foreclosures or short sales. These are techniques, how to do something. In my opinion, that's the small picture. Techniques are important, but they are more training than education.

Kim and I created the *CASHFLOW* games—101, 202, and *CASHFLOW for Kids*—in board games as well as online versions to make available the fun, experiential, simple, and big-picture vision of the world of money.

I use the word "fun" because getting rich is fun once you learn the game. Games make learning fun and, as the Cone of Learning illustrates, simulation—which is what the *CASHFLOW* games are—is one of the best ways to learn something new and retain what you learn.

In *Unfair Advantage,* I used the example of the game of golf, a frustrating game when you first start to play. But after taking lessons, practicing, playing regularly, and challenging yourself in tournaments, it can be fun. Most avid golfers say, "The game keeps you coming back."

Although I do not always win in the game of money, it's the game that keeps me coming back. It's fun, challenging, ever-changing, and profitable. Most importantly, once I began to win, I never needed to worry about job security or if I would have enough money for retirement. I earn more money, pay less in taxes, and have the freedom to do what I want with my time.

The Foundation of an Unfair Advantage

CASHFLOW 101 will teach you fundamental investing.

Profession _____   **Player** _____

Goal: Get out of the Rat Race and onto the Fast Track by building up your **Passive Income** to be **greater** than your **Total Expenses**

INCOME STATEMENT

INCOME

Description	Cash Flow
Salary:	
Interest/Dividends:	
Real Estate/Business:	

Auditor _____

(Person on your right)

Passive Income : $ _____
(Cash Flow from
Interest/Dividends +
Real Estate/Business)

Total
Income: $ _____

EXPENSES

Taxes:	
Home Mortgage Payment:	
School Loan Payment:	
Car Loan Payment:	
Credit Card Payment:	
Retail Payment:	
Other Expenses:	
Child Expenses:	
Loan Payment:	

Number of
Children: _____
(Begin game with 0 Children)

Per Child $ _____
Expense:

**Total
Expenses:** $ _____

BALANCE SHEET

Monthly Cash Flow (PAYCHECK)**:** $ _____
(Total Income - Total Expenses)

ASSETS

Savings:		
Stocks/Funds/CDs:	# of Shares:	Cost/Share:
Real Estate/Business:	Down Pay:	Cost:

LIABILITIES

Home Mortgage:	
School Loans:	
Car Loans:	
Credit Cards:	
Retail Debt:	
Real Estate/Business:	Mortgage/Liability:
Loan:	

CASHFLOW 202 teaches technical investing.

CASHFLOW 202				Player_____	Auditor_____			
OPTIONS WORKSHEET								
Call Options *(You expect the stock price to go up.)*								
Stock Symbol	# of Shares (a)	Cost of Option/Share (b)	Total Amt. Paid (a x b)	Strike Price (c)	Today's New Price (d)	Price Gain (d – c)	Amount Receive (d – c) x a	Turn Count
								1 2 3
								1 2 3
								1 2 3
								1 2 3
								1 2 3
								1 2 3
Put Options *(You expect the stock price to go down.)*								
Stock Symbol	# of Shares (a)	Cost of Option/Share (b)	Total Amt. Paid (a x b)	Strike Price (c)	Today's New Price (d)	Price Gain (c – d)	Amount Receive (c – d) x a	Turn Count
								1 2 3
								1 2 3
								1 2 3
								1 2 3
								1 2 3
								1 2 3

Turn Count: To keep track of your 3 turns before your options expire, mark off each number as that number turn passes.

SHORT SALES WORKSHEET *(You expect the stock price to go down.)*						
Stock Symbol	# of Shares (a)	Sale Price Per Share (b)	Total Sales Amount (a x b)	Cost Per Share (c)	Total Cost (a x c)	Total Gain/Loss (a x b) – (a x c)

For examples of how to record your Call Options, Put Options and Short Sales, please refer to pages 6, 7 and 10 in the CASHFLOW 202 rule book.

As you know from reading this book, fundamental investors invest for cash flow, and technical Investors invest for capital gains. And as you also now know, cash flow is taxed at a lower rate than capital gains. Most investment courses, such as stock trading, real estate flipping, or currency trading, focus on capital-gains investing. The

CASHFLOW games, *101* and *202,* teach you to invest for both capital gains and cash flow.

Knowing how to invest for both capital gains and cash flow is the foundation of an unfair advantage in the real markets.

Quantum Leaps in Learning

After playing the *CASHFLOW* games multiple times with other like-minded people and learning the fundamental Rich Dad principles, you will experience a leap in understanding due to the Law of Compensation #3: the power of compounding education.

If you believe you are ready to move on, you may want to assist in teaching others and supporting the leader of your local CASHFLOW club. You may even want to become a CASHFLOW club leader and start your own club.

When you teach, you will find your understanding, once again, takes a quantum leap. This is due to the Law of Compensation #1: the power of reciprocity. Give, and you shall receive.

Basic and Advanced Programs

After this foundational learning, you may be ready to decide which asset class is best for you. As you already know, there are four basic asset classes:

1. Business/Entrepreneurship
2. Real estate
3. Paper assets
4. Commodities.

Rich Dad offers programs in entrepreneurship, real estate, and trading paper assets. We do not offer courses in commodities, such as gold and silver, simply because it does not require much financial education to buy or sell gold and silver.

When I invest in oil, I invest as an entrepreneur. Oil exploration is a complex investment.

In my opinion, entrepreneurship requires the highest level of financial education. Entrepreneurs are also the richest people in the world.

Real estate requires the second highest level of financial education.

Paper assets are the easiest to get into. You can invest with a few dollars—or millions of dollars. Paper assets are also the riskiest of the asset classes, especially in a volatile economy.

Commodities require the least financial education. If you invest in precious metals such as gold and silver, all you have to know is how much money central banks are printing and how much debt the country you live in is carrying. In the United States, gold and silver have been a good investment since 1998. All you have to do is buy and hold.

How long the precious-metals market will remain a good market for investors will depend upon the actions of our world leaders. If our leaders do a good job, gold and silver will decline in value. If our leaders are incompetent, gold and silver will go through the roof.

Courses and Coaching

The Rich Dad Company offers educational courses and coaching programs through Rich Dad Coaching and Rich Dad Education. You can learn more about these programs, and CASHFLOW clubs, at RichDad.com.

Which Programs Are Best for You?

Which courses are best for you depends upon you.

When I returned from Vietnam in 1973, my rich dad recommended that I take a basic real estate investment course because I needed to learn how to manage and profit from debt. Since the dollar was backed by debt, he said that learning about debt was essential to my basic financial education.

When I told him that I was interested in becoming an entrepreneur, he suggested I take formal courses in sales. In 1974, I joined the Xerox Corporation because they had the best sales-training program. I stayed with Xerox for four years until I became #1 in sales.

Today, I am a best-selling author, not a "best-writing" author.

I also recommend technical investing, such as our course which teaches futures and commodities trading, because all markets go up and down and all markets have a past, present, and a future.

My financial education never stops because my financial education is my unfair advantage.

Bonus FAQ #2: Do I Need a Coach?

FAQ
When do you hire a coach?

Short Answer
When something is important to you.

Explanation
Professionals have coaches and amateurs do not.

Superman and Wonder Woman exist only in comic books. The rest of us are human beings.

All professional athletes have coaches. They may be talented, but they know they are not Supermen or Wonder Women.

I know I am not Superman. If I were, I could do everything I wanted. Life would be easy.

And while I may not be Superman, I know I have untapped power and potential. I know I need to be pushed if I want to access that power and maximize my potential.

When I know I need to be pushed, held accountable, challenged to go beyond my resistance, my laziness, my limitations, I hire a coach—if what I want is important to me.

Recently a close friend died. He was a young man. He was a great guy and very successful in every area of his life, except his health. Rather than hire a coach, change his diet, and stop drinking, he simply worked harder. He, like so many, let his health deteriorate while he focused on earning more and more money. Today he is dead, leaving behind a young wife and two kids.

I was on the same path. After age 35, I exercised less, ate more, drank more, and worked harder. It was not long before I had gained 60 pounds.

Rather than hire a coach, I kept saying, "I'll go on a diet tomorrow. I'll exercise tomorrow. I'll fit in my old clothes in a month." The problem was, tomorrow came and went. And my weight kept increasing.

One day, sitting at my desk, I saw a picture of Kim and me at the beach. I was embarrassed. Kim looked beautiful, smiling and loving, and I was twice her size, my gut filling most of the picture. That is when I knew I needed to stop kidding myself and hire a coach.

I worked out with a number of fitness coaches. Finally, I found one of the toughest coaches in town and that made all the difference. Not only does he hold me accountable, but he pushes me as hard as he pushes his 20- and 30-year-olds. There is no mercy for age. This is important to me because I found myself making excuses for my age. For my coach, age is not an excuse. That's the kind of coach I needed.

Today, in my sixties, I am healthier than I was in my forties and fifties. My weight still goes up and down, but it is not out of control. Most importantly, as I progress into my sixties, I am actually working harder at keeping fit and healthy than I did when I was in my thirties, because I have to. Working out was easy in my thirties. My sixties have presented greater challenges.

I did not hire a coach just for health. My health is important, but not as important as my life with Kim. She makes my life worth living and I want to enjoy this gift of life with her in great health.

So the question is: What is important to you? It's not just money or health. It's the things that money and good health can mean to you and your family. Money affects all the things that are important in our lives. I remember feeling embarrassed and angry with myself when Kim and I were flat broke. I felt I had let her down, so I sought help from a coach to speed up my financial recovery.

If you are ready to change quadrants, from E to S, or S to B, I would hire a coach. Changing quadrants is not easy for most people. Any important change is never easy, so a coach is essential when you are serious about changing your life.

Remember that, when deciding which asset class is best for you, it's not just real estate, or entrepreneurship, or paper assets that are important. It is what being successful as an entrepreneur or real estate investor means to you. When you decide what is most important to you, then it's time to hire a coach.

Bonus FAQ #3: What if I'm Deep in Debt?

FAQ
I am deeply in debt. Will your financial education programs help me?

Short Answer
Probably not.

Explanation
There is good debt and bad debt. Bad debt is nasty. Bad debt is why the economies of the United States and many countries around the world are stagnant, depressed, and dying.

For obvious reasons, I would love to have you purchase Rich Dad's advanced education and coaching programs. But bad debt is a sign of deeper problems, sometimes emotional ones. Bad debt is often just the tip of the iceberg.

Rather than sign up for our financial education and coaching programs, especially the advanced programs, I would recommend you join a CASHFLOW club and play the game with like-minded people a number of times. That experience will help you discover the true reasons that cause you to be deeply in debt. Once you have a better understanding of your situation and its causes, you will be able to make better decisions about your financial future.

Emotions are the biggest cause of financial problems. As Warren Buffett often says, "If you cannot control your emotions, you cannot control your money."

Years ago, when I was nearly $1 million in debt, Kim and I created a program we used to get out of bad debt. We needed to get out of bad debt—so that we could get into good debt. To learn more about this product, *How We Got Out of Bad Debt,* visit RichDad.com.

Bonus FAQ #4: How Do I Start?

FAQ
How do I start? I don't have much money.

Short Answer
Get a job. Do something.

Explanation
When I was young, I was taught: "God helps those who help themselves."

Too many people want help, but are unwilling to help themselves or others. Too many people allow the excuse, "I don't have any money," to stop them.

It takes no special talent to say, "I don't have any money." Anyone can do it and millions of people do. In the real world of money, ambition is far more important than your education. The primary reasons people lack money are first, the lack of ambition, and second, the lack of education. If you cannot find the ambition to make some money, financial education will probably not help you.

In Hawaii, there is a 15-year old boy who rides his bike after school to the bus stop, loads his bike on the bus and rides an hour to town. When he arrives, he unloads his bike and rides to where his CASHFLOW club meets. After the meeting, he rides his bike back to the bus stop, loads his bike on the bus, and rides an hour to the bus stop nearest his home where he unloads his bike and rides home.

I have no doubt this young man will be successful in anything he does in life.

Bonus FAQ #5: Is There a Program for Me?

FAQ
I'm a pretty sophisticated investor. Will your programs help me?

Short Answer
Probably not.

Explanation
Our education and coaching programs are for people who want to learn, not for people who think they know all the answers. In the recent financial crisis, millions of people lost trillions of dollars following the advice of people who knew all the answers.

You may recall that the leaders of Enron were often referred to as "the smartest guys in the room." Today, Enron is gone and the employees of and investors in Enron are also gone.

Remember Lehman Brothers? Lehman was run by really smart men and women, many from our best schools. Today, they're gone, too.

Merrill Lynch, the stock-brokerage house advising millions of clients, was on the verge of going bust before they were saved by Bank of America.

And what about all the financial gurus on TV? They're really smart people. Why didn't they tell the world to get out of the stock market? Why are they still giving financial advice today?

Then there's Ben Bernanke. How can the Federal Reserve Bank Chairman say (on June 9, 2010), "I don't fully understand movements in the gold price?" If he controls the most powerful bank in the world, isn't he supposed to be one of the smartest people in the world?

Even if you made millions between 2007 and 2010, you can still learn more.

The period between 2007 and 2010 were the best years of my investing career. I made millions, and I know I can still learn more.

I plan on learning more because it is my financial education, not my college education, that is my unfair advantage.

Always remember that the difference between the top 20 golfers in America and the top 120 is less than two strokes, less than one stroke per round. The top 20 make millions. The bottom 100 earn a comfortable living. No professional golfer can afford to say they know everything. Even though they've putted a million balls a million times, they know they can still learn more about putting.

Professionals know it is sometimes the smallest things that can give them their biggest unfair advantage.

Bonus FAQ #6: Are There Programs for Entrepreneurs?

FAQ
What programs do you have for entrepreneurs?

Short Answer
Rich Dad has many programs for entrepreneurs.

Ultimately, all of our programs are designed for entrepreneurs. There are entrepreneurs in business, in real estate, in paper assets, and in precious metals. They are people who take control of their money and their financial future.

If you are not an entrepreneur, you probably have a job, work for money, save your money, and turn your retirement money over to strangers.

Explanation
Building a business into an asset takes the highest degree of financial education. Since the world needs more entrepreneurs to create more jobs, we at Rich Dad are developing a program called GEO. GEO stands for Global Entrepreneurs Organization. It is, without a doubt, our most dynamic and ambitious undertaking ever, and it is for people who are entrepreneurs or want to be entrepreneurs. We expect that GEO will be a three-year program that will train people to become entrepreneurs the Rich Dad way.

FAQ

Will it teach me to build my business?

Short Answer

No.

Explanation

GEO will train people to be entrepreneurs. Once their training is complete, they can start to build their business.

FAQ

What if I want to build my business while I am being trained?

Short Answer

Then the program may not be right for you.

Explanation

I went to flight school to learn to be a pilot. I did not become a pilot until after I finished flight school.

Doctors do not become doctors until after they finish medical school. After medical school, they become interns or resident doctors, still in training. Not all students finish flight school. Not all students finish medical school.

If I had said to the Marine Corps, "I want to fly fighter jets the first day of flight school," I would have been released immediately for mental and emotional delusion. The same is true for business. Many people get so caught up in the idea of starting a business ("being my own boss") that they forget the critical need for formal training. Small wonder that nine out of 10 new businesses fail within the first five years.

If you want to take the risk and believe you can beat the odds and become the one in 10 that succeeds, give it your best shot. The GEO program is probably not for you.

It was only after I was awarded my wings that I was allowed to choose the aircraft I wanted to fly. I knew I was not cut out to be a fighter pilot or a transport pilot. I chose helicopter gunships. It was one of the smartest decisions of my life. Once I knew how to fly, I then knew what I wanted to fly.

The gunship fit my personality. I wanted an unfair advantage: air versus ground… a helicopter-gunship pilot versus a soldier on the ground.

FAQ
But what if I have a great idea for a new product or business?

Short Answer
That is where the delusion begins.

Explanation
Pictured below is the B-I Triangle, the 8 Integrities of a Business.

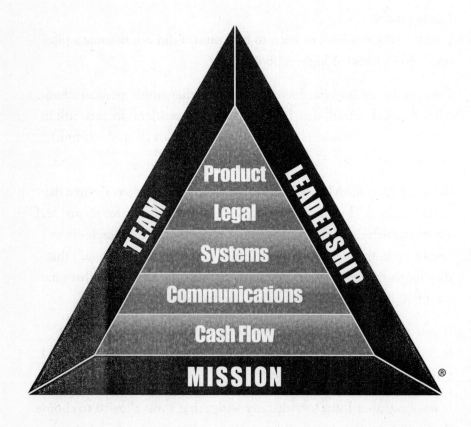

Notice the eight components that make up the B-I Triangle. You can see that "product" is the smallest integrity of the triangle. That is because the product or service is the least important part of any business.

The product is just the tip of the iceberg. It is the lower part of an iceberg, what's below the surface, that sinks big ships.

Whenever I have someone say to me, "But I have a great product or great idea," I know they do not see the iceberg. That's what sunk the *Titanic* and what sinks most businesses, big or small, old and new.

The GEO program is being designed to teach you to put a complete business together, making sure that the eight integrities are working together and to your advantage in building a strong and profitable business. Putting the eight integrities of a business together is what successful entrepreneurs do.

Once an entrepreneur knows how to put together the eight integrities, they are better able to build a business around any product or service.

FAQ

What are the "8 Integrities of a Business"?

Short Answer

I wish I had a short answer but I don't have one. So I will simply explain what each of the eight integrities stands for.

Mission

Mission is at the base of the B-I Triangle because it is the foundation, the business's reason for existence.

A mission comes from the heart of the entrepreneur. A mission goes far beyond just making money.

There are two kinds of entrepreneurs. *Transformational entrepreneurs* want to change the world. Steve Jobs of Apple falls into this category. This is why he is a designer and innovator. *Transactional entrepreneurs* want to beat their competition, drive down prices, and make money. Most entrepreneurs fall into this category. I operate in both categories.

Team

A successful business is made up of a team of different people with different professions. Great teams have professionals (such as lawyers and accountants) people with different skills (PR, marketing, sales), different talents (marketing, graphic design, copywriting, web design), different experience (years of work and varied backgrounds) and different expectations. Rich dad often said, "Business is easy. Working with people is hard."

This is why most entrepreneurs fail to build a business. They are lone rangers, or lone wolves, working by themselves or with fewer than 20 people. They do not build a business. They own a job.

Leadership

The leader, the entrepreneur, focuses people and resources in order to produce a result on time and on budget. The leader of an organization is responsible for the successful integration that's needed for all eight integrities to operate together.

Leaders employ specialists such as lawyers, accountants, and web designers. Specialists know a lot about a very specific topic or area — generally only one of the eight integrities. Leaders know a little about a lot. And they must know a little about each of the eight integrities.

One reason why so many people fail as entrepreneurs is because they leave school overly specialized in only one of the eight integrities and lacking in generalized business knowledge and skills, especially leadership skills.

Looking at the B-I Triangle, you will see...

...the outer integrities: mission, team, and leadership. This is what military schools teach.

One reason I do well as an entrepreneur, even though I did not go to a traditional business school, is because of my military school training. The first day at the Merchant Marine Academy, we had to memorize the mission of the school. The next day we began learning to become leaders and to operate as teams.

Today, I hire graduates of traditional business, accounting and law schools, specialists who are much smarter and better trained in business than I am.

Military school gave me an unfair advantage over graduates of traditional schools in the world of entrepreneurship. In the corporate world, business-school graduates have an unfair advantage over me. That is fine with me because I have never wanted to live in the corporate world.

This is why GEO puts such an emphasis on mission, team and leadership. If you are a strong leader, you can hire people smarter and better trained than you are.

Cash Flow

The cash flow of a business is often managed by a CFO, chief financial officer, an accountant or a bookkeeper. Cash flow is just above mission and is often called "the bottom line."

If the leader has done a great job, there should be plenty of cash flow for salaries, profits, dividends, and capital to keep the business going forward.

If the leader has done a bad job, there are cash shortages, cutbacks, layoffs, and diminishing working capital.

Communications

Communications is positioned just above the cash-flow section of the B-I Triangle because communications, both internal and external, directly impacts cash flow—both positively and negatively.

There are external communications to customers, often called PR (public relations), marketing, advertising, and sales. There are internal communications to employees, suppliers, management, and shareholders. Organizations with poor internal and external communications suffer in all eight integrities, especially the bottom line.

Sales are included in communications. Sales equal income. One reason why so many new entrepreneurs fail is because they cannot sell enough to cover the costs of running a business and the cost of their personal living expenses.

Sales training and development will be an essential component of GEO. If you cannot sell or do not like selling, you should not become an entrepreneur.

In 1973, when I returned from Vietnam, my rich dad told me to start looking for someone to train me to sell. That is why I went to work for Xerox for four years, *before* starting my first business.

The most important skill of an entrepreneur is the ability to raise capital. If an entrepreneur cannot sell, the business will die. And the primary reason most businesses fail to get off the ground is because the entrepreneur cannot raise capital.

Learning how to raise capital is another important component of GEO programs.

As a member of GEO, you will learn to be excellent at PR, marketing, and sales. Simply put, if you are excellent at PR and marketing, sales will come easily. If you are weak at PR and marketing, sales will be tough and you will have to sell hard. Learning to communicate to your customers and to your staff the Rich Dad way is an important part of GEO.

Systems

A business is a system of systems, just as a car or the human body is a system of systems.

A car has a fuel system, ignition system, brake system, hydraulic system, steering system, and many other systems. If one system goes out, the car struggles to function or stops running completely.

The human body has the circulatory system, respiratory system, digestive system, skeletal system, nervous system and more. Like a car, if one system is weak or out of order, the entire body suffers or stops functioning.

A business is the same as a car or a body. It is a system of systems, including phone systems, web systems, accounting systems, marketing systems, legal systems, production systems, and distribution systems. Like a car or a body, if one of the systems is out or damaged, the business falters or dies.

For example, let's say the business is strong, but accounting systems and processes are weak. It will not be long before the business suffers due to shoddy record keeping, poor reporting, unpaid (or overpaid) taxes, and ultimately, a lack of cash flow.

Learning to manage accounting and reporting systems will be an important part of GEO.

Legal

Contracts, agreements, and knowledge of the laws are essential to business success.

Legal agreements create and define assets. For example, when I write a book, the legal contracts turn the book into an asset, a piece of intellectual property. Without legal agreements, it would be nearly impossible to do business on a global scale.

Real estate is a mass of legal agreements. The same is true for trading stocks and raising capital. Without legal agreements and respect for the law, there would be chaos.

Your relationships and agreements with the employees of your business or the tenants in your rental units are also defined by legal contracts.

Many entrepreneurs build a great business and wind up turning over their hard-earned money to an attorney because of stupid mistakes the entrepreneur did not know he or she had made.

Legal is an important component of any entrepreneurial venture. It is near the top of the B-I Triangle to remind you to have sound processes and systems in place for agreements—and a good attorney to guide you.

Product

The least important integrity is product. This does not mean products aren't important or should not be of the highest quality. Products are important from the consumer's point of view. The business that delivers the product is important to the entrepreneur and investors in the business.

I believe everyone has a million-dollar idea or product. The problem is that they lack the entrepreneurial skills and talents to turn their idea into a million-dollar business.

From the B/I perspective, the business is far more important than the product. The product is just a product. The business is the asset.

FAQ

Aren't we all capitalists?

Short Answer

No.

Explanation

In the communist world, there are doctors, lawyers, bankers, pilots, web designers, and teachers. These are the people who make up any economy, regardless if it is capitalist, socialist, or communist.

True capitalists are people who use other people's labor and other people's money to do what people and governments want done. They use capital markets and enrich themselves in the process. If you work for money and invest your money, you are part of a capitalist society, but not necessarily a capitalist.

The definition of capitalism is: An economic system in which the means of production are privately owned and operated for a private profit.

Karl Marx defined the proletariat, the working class, as people who do not own the means of production. When schools train you to get a job or work for money as an accountant, lawyer, or doctor, you are being trained to work for a capitalist. Rich Dad's three-year GEO program is being developed to train you to become a capitalist.

Bonus FAQ #7: Is Entrepreneurship for Everyone?

FAQ

Can anyone be an entrepreneur?

Short Answer

Yes. A young boy in my neighborhood mows lawns on weekends. He is an entrepreneur.

Being an entrepreneur is no big deal. Being a successful entrepreneur *is* a big deal.

Studies show that many entrepreneurs earn less than their employees when you compare the gross dollars earned and the number of hours put into the business.

Explanation

Since being an entrepreneur is no big deal, a better question to ask might be, "What kind of entrepreneur do I want to be?"

There is an old Chinese proverb that comes to mind: "In the forest, there are many different birds."

If you look at the CASHFLOW Quadrant, think of each quadrant as a different forest, and in that forest are varieties of different birds. The following sections illustrate this point.

The E Quadrant

In this forest is a wide variety of different employees, from CEOs to janitors, lawyers to laborers, accountants to tax evaders, managers and mothers.

There are employees who work full-time, part-time, by the hour, on commission, or for a monthly salary. There are those who work from home, work in an office, or work from anywhere.

The S Quadrant

In the S quadrant forest lives another wide variety of birds. The S quadrant is where most entrepreneurs roost. S stands for small business, businesses with fewer than 500 employees. S also stands for smart person: doctors, lawyers or consultants with a small business built around special skills.

Here are a few more plays on the letter S:

- **S stands for selfish person.** They are small and stay small because they do not want to share what they earn. They do everything, from answering the phone, to cleaning the office, to doing their own taxes.

- **S stands for stupid.** There are many successful entrepreneurs who are successful in spite of themselves. There are others who are stupid and stubborn and no one else will hire them, so they work by themselves.

- **S stands for star.** This person could be a recording artist, movie star, or sports figure. They usually sell their star power to the highest bidder.

- **S stands for strange.** Many artists or eccentric people gravitate to the S quadrant. They need to be who they are, do their own thing, and strut their stuff. Most do not fit into the normal world and have no plans to try to fit in. The brave new world of the web is filled with strange birds, people doing strange things, begging for attention.

- **S also stands for self-employed.** Most entrepreneurs are self-employed. They do not own a business. They own a job. They cannot stop working because, if they stopped working, their income would stop.

  Once a self-employed person can leave their business—and the business does better without them—they have become a true entrepreneur. They have built an asset, which is what true entrepreneurs do.

The B Quadrant

B means big business, a business with more than 500 employees and big corporate offices.

Most B-quadrant businesses operate via corporate offices and branch offices.

I have found that managers who work for big public companies are different from managers who work for entrepreneurial private businesses. One reason I was anxious to leave the Xerox Corporation was because I did not like the type of managers they hired to manage the workers. A corporate culture is different from an entrepreneurial culture.

There are many different ways to create an entrepreneurial-business asset in the B quadrant.

- **Franchising**

  Franchisors sell the rights to do business with their corporate entity. McDonalds is one of the best-known examples of franchising.

- **Licensing**

  An agreement to license allows another business to do business with your business. This is the Rich Dad business model. We have a small corporate office, but license our intellectual property to businesses throughout the world.

  Through licensing agreements, Rich Dad has thousands of people all over the world, working to promote and sell our products, seminars, and educational programs.

- **Network marketing**

  Network marketing is a business system that can expand infinitely. A single person can start with very little money and expand into a worldwide business with thousands of people working together to build their independent businesses.

  There are hundreds of millions of people around the world involved in this type of business.

The I Quadrant

I stands for investor, those who understand the art and science of raising capital. When you can build a business in the B quadrant and raise capital, you are a capitalist.

- **Bank financing**

  When you borrow money from a bank to invest in real estate, you are operating in the I quadrant. This is why rich dad insisted I take classes on real estate, not just to learn about real estate and taxes, but to learn to manage debt. Today, I have hundreds of millions of dollars in good debt, all producing income for me—most of it tax-free.

If you use debt to finance your home or car, you are a consumer, not a capitalist.

- **IPO**

  In *Unfair Advantage,* I wrote about taking a company public through an IPO, an initial public offering. Taking a company public was my goal when I started out to become an entrepreneur. It took me 30 years. It was a tough process, but I learned a lot and grew up in the process.

  To qualify to raise capital via an IPO, the securities market must be assured that you have a B-quadrant business or have the ability to build a B-quadrant business.

- **Private placements**

  Obviously, private is opposite from public. The term "private placement" is used when offering the sale of a security that doesn't involve an offering to the public. Private placements are used for raising small amounts of money or for raising money from a few qualified investors. Private placements are not for the general public.

  The general public invests in "common shares," securities deemed safe enough for the uneducated, unsophisticated public.

  When I was in my twenties and thirties, I used a number of private placements to raise capital for oil and gas partnerships. I did it more for the experience than the money. I worked long and hard, earning very little, but learning a lot.

  Today, what I learned years ago makes me a lot of money in oil and gas partnerships, validating the Laws of Compensation and the power of compounding education.

- **Franchise offering**
  A franchise offering is also a security and follows strict rules and regulations. A franchisor allows a franchisee to use their product or service, brand, trademarks, systems, advertising, and trade secrets. Again, McDonalds uses a franchise model to grow their business. McDonalds also uses the stock market to raise additional capital.

  I have never completed a successful franchise offering and would like to someday, primarily for the experience. Launching a franchise is a much more sophisticated venture than an IPO because a franchisee sells a turnkey business, often to people who are not entrepreneurs. Creating a business that can be run profitably by the average person is a monumental task.

FAQ
Will I learn about the B quadrant and I quadrant in GEO?

Short Answer
Yes. That is the purpose in creating GEO.

Explanation
The world is filled with E's and S's. The world needs more B's and I's, which is why Rich Dad is creating GEO. The first step in becoming an entrepreneur is to learn how to build a true asset in the S quadrant.

Remember, most people in the S quadrant are self-employed. They cannot stop working because their business is not an asset that can run without them. Once the person has built a sustainable asset in the S quadrant, they may decide to move on to the challenges of the B quadrant.

FAQ
In the GEO program, does a person have to move on to the B and I quadrants?

Short Answer
No.

Explanation
A person can stop anytime. I suspect most people will be very happy with a business in the S quadrant.

FAQ
Why wouldn't a person go on to the B and I quadrants?

Short Answer
Each quadrant presents its own challenges and the going gets harder as you move into the B and I quadrants. Success on the right side of the CASHFLOW Quadrant requires more education and dedication, and greater leadership skills.

Explanation
As I stated earlier, I went to flight school to become a pilot. I did not become a pilot until I finished flight school. Once I completed my training, then I chose the aircraft I wanted to fly. As the performance of my aircraft increased, so did the requirements related to my skill level—especially in combat situations.

The same process of skill, training and educational development is involved in GEO. Start small in the S quadrant and learn the skills to be a successful entrepreneur. You can then decide to move on to the B quadrant and then to the I quadrant. Or you can stop and start your own business.

Some may find that moving into the S quadrant proves to be too challenging. While anyone can be an entrepreneur, becoming an entrepreneur is not for everyone.

FAQ
Do I have to quit my job to join the GEO program?

Short Answer
No.

Explanation
As I have often said, "Keep your daytime job and start a part-time business." The reason most small businesses fail in the first five years

is because the fledgling entrepreneur cannot earn enough money to support the business, themselves, and their families. Learning to become an entrepreneur takes time.

FAQ

Why won't most people move to the B quadrant and then to the I quadrant?

Short Answer

It's not easy. Changing quadrants means an increase in knowledge and personal discipline.

Explanation

Most people become entrepreneurs because they want to "do their own thing" or "do things their way." Even if profitable, the business they create is often too dependent upon the unique talents of the entrepreneur and fails to evolve into a business.

The reason the B-I Triangle is called "The 8 Integrities of a Business" is because the definition of the word *integrity* is whole, or complete.

S-Quadrant Doctor

Let me give you an example. I have a doctor friend who is a genius, a magician. He is also a loner. He answers his own phone, makes his own appointments, does his own taxes, and cleans his own office.

Since he has very few expenses, he makes a lot of money. The problem is, he is the entire B-I Triangle for his business. He is the business. He is so smart that he has the ability to do the tasks of many people. But he cannot stop working because, if he does, his cash flow stops.

While this is an extreme example, the world is filled with self-employed entrepreneurs like my doctor.

Although he was a genius in medical school and does well in private practice, he is stuck in the S quadrant, with little hope of building that business into a B-quadrant business or continuing on to the I quadrant. He is an S-quadrant doctor.

B-Quadrant Doctor

There is another doctor I know who does not see patients. In spite of that fact, he affects the well-being of thousands of patients each year. Rather than spending his time one-on-one with patients, he spends his time building hospitals. He has hospitals in the United States and China.

Because he can build profitable hospitals that employ thousands of people, he receives giant tax breaks and is able to raise money from rich private investors as well as public investors through Wall Street via publicly-traded stocks. This doctor operates in the B and I quadrants.

His B-I Triangles are hospitals, which operate in integrity. This means that the eight integrities of the B-I Triangle operate synergistically, whole and complete, and in compliance legally, ethically, and morally.

This is what GEO will teach and train entrepreneurs to do. As you become a successful entrepreneur, you can build businesses around any product or service you choose. Keep in mind that the product is the least important part of the triangle. Once an entrepreneur knows how to build a B-I Triangle, the products or services are interchangeable. Today, I am an entrepreneur in education, real estate, gold, silver, media, and oil.

FAQ
Which quadrant is the hardest?

Short Answer
They all are… at the start.

Anything is difficult if you do not know how to do it. Take walking for example. A baby struggles to learn to stand, falling down many times. Yet once they learn to stand, they want to walk, then run. Once a baby knows how to run, he or she can take on the world.

Explanation
I recommend starting in the S quadrant, then moving to the B, and then the I quadrant. It is the same process as a baby learning to stand, then walk, then run.

FAQ
Why don't most entrepreneurs make it to the B and I quadrants?

Short Answer
Lack of discipline.

Explanation
Success requires discipline. More success requires more discipline. Most entrepreneurs want to do their own thing or do things their way, so they never make it out of the S quadrant.

The B quadrant requires more rules and more discipline.

The most disciplined quadrant is the I quadrant. It has the most rules and the least freedom.

FAQ
Why does the I quadrant have the least freedom?

Short Answer
Because you're using OPM, other people's money.

Government regulations are extremely strict when you use OPM. In the United States, there are agencies like the SEC, the Securities and Exchange Commission, that regulate and monitor I-quadrant activity.

FAQ
Is the I quadrant where you find most of the financial corruption?

Short Answer
Yes.

Explanation
The I quadrant breeds financial corruption.

This is where Bernie Madoff lived. He was never really a B-quadrant entrepreneur. He was an I- quadrant entrepreneur, a guy who pulled off the second-biggest Ponzi scheme in history. The biggest Ponzi scheme of all time, in my opinion, is the U.S. government's Social Security program, also an I-quadrant scam.

Many small entrepreneurs break the laws of the I quadrant out of ignorance. They raise money when they do not yet have a business — when they have no business raising money.

Simply put, if you are going to raise money in the I quadrant, it is best that you know how to build a sustainable business in the S or B quadrant before raising capital. This is also why rich dad required me to take real estate investment courses. He wanted me to practice using a banker's money to fund my real estate business. He wanted me to use a bank's money before I used OPM, money from friends and family, to fund my businesses.

As rich dad often said, "When you lose a person's money, you lose a part of their life."

Once I learned to raise money from bankers for real estate investments, I began raising funds for oil and gas limited partnerships via PPM, private placement memorandums. I did this in the 1970s and 1980s.

In 2004, I sold my first business via an IPO, an initial public offering. I went from bankers' money, to private offerings to public offerings. It was all part of my financial education in the I quadrant.

FAQ
Will I learn to raise capital in GEO?

Short Answer
It depends.

Explanation
Remember: You should know how to build S- and B-quadrant businesses before raising capital in the I quadrant.

There are many people who are so desperate for money that they focus on the I quadrant, and not the S or the B quadrant. This is why frauds, scams, and rip-offs abound in the financial world.

These people want to raise money, but are not entrepreneurs.

Before we will teach people about the I quadrant, Rich Dad wants to make sure the person is a well-trained, disciplined, ethical, and moral entrepreneur. If you know how to build a B-quadrant business, money from the I quadrant will find you.

Bonus FAQ #8: What's the Big Win?

FAQ
What is the greatest benefit from Rich Dad's financial education?

Short Answer
An unfair advantage.

Explanation
There are two unfair advantages:

1. You won't be a financial victim.
2. You can be part of the solution.

The financial crisis that began in 2007 is not over. We are in the eye of the storm and I believe that the heart of this crisis is still coming.

Don't Be a Victim

In *Rich Dad's Prophecy*, published in 2002, I stated that a perfect storm is brewing. Unfortunately, in 2011 as I write this book, the storm is getting bigger and much more powerful. The storm grows bigger because our leaders in government, the banking industry, and Wall Street are not solving the problem. They are making the problem worse.

Rather than solve the problem, our leaders continue to play games with money: printing trillions of dollars, dropping interest rates to near zero in the hope that more people will borrow more money, increasing national debt rather than increasing production, propping up the stock market and housing markets, and lying to the naïve, the financially uneducated, and the gullible.

In 1963, while I was in high school, Bob Dylan sang the song, "The Times They Are A-Changin'."

As a kid, I did not know what was changing, but in my gut I knew something was, and the lyrics rang true.

Unfortunately, most people want things to go back to "normal." They expect the clouds to clear, the sun to break through, and the birds to sing… with jobs and pay raises bouncing back and the economy growing at 10 percent a year. Most people are hoping their political leaders, the government, our schools, and financial institutions will solve our problems. Millions of American seem to believe that throwing the bums out of Washington will solve their problems.

I am not as optimistic. It's not that our leaders, new or old, are necessarily bad people. It's just that the financial problem has grown too big, beyond the control of our government and our leaders. How much power does the President really have when we owe the world so much money? How does the United States tell China what to do when they have so much of our money? How does the United States influence the world when the world has lost faith in the dollar?

To make matters worse, this global loss of confidence in America comes at a time when our internal financial problems are about to explode.

In 2010, baby boomers began collecting Social Security, and Social Security is broke. Medicare, an even bigger sinkhole in the U.S. budget, is expected to "go broke" by 2019. In spite of Social Security and Medicare insolvency, our President signed a healthcare reform bill into law, adding further stress to social and financial problems.

And the United States continues to fight two wars on two fronts, wars we cannot win. We cannot win because we do not fight industrialized nations as we did in World War II. All we have to do is replace the words "Iraq" and "Afghanistan" with "Vietnam," a war in which I fought, and people would understand the insanity of these two wars.

Definition of Crisis

One of the definitions of the word "crisis" is: "A crucial stage or turning point in the course of something." In a medical context: "After the crisis, the patient either dies or gets better."

You and I are at a turning point in world history. The question is: Will we die or get better?

There are many people who ask, "Is the economy coming back?" My reply is, "The economy has moved on."

Without financial education, most people cannot move on.

Rather than move on, they live in the past, clinging to financial values that are obsolete. Many parents still tell their children to "Go to school to get a good job" at a time when jobs are fluid, moving to the lowest-labor-cost countries. They continue to advise their kids to "Save money" at a time when central banks are printing trillions. And many continue to stuff money into their retirement plans at the exact moment in history when millions of baby boomers begin withdrawing their money from their retirement plans.

As I predicted in *Rich Dad's Prophecy*, the perfect financial storm is still coming.

Rather than be a victim, you can take the initiative to improve your financial education—a move that gives you the unfair advantage of training your mind to see this time of economic crisis and turmoil as an opportunity to get further ahead, rather than fall behind and have your wealth ripped from you.

You Can Change the Future

Your second unfair advantage is that you can be part of the solution to the challenges that our world faces.

The financial crisis of 2007 actually began a long time ago. It started in 1913 when the Federal Reserve Bank was created. In 1913, the Internal Revenue Service was also created when the Sixteenth Amendment to the U.S. Constitution was ratified. Both acts violated the spirit of the Constitution of the United States.

Was this a coincidence? I doubt it.

In 2011, money is no longer money. Money stopped being money in 1971. Today, money is debt.

Today, for every dollar printed, the IRS must tax the taxpayer to pay for the principal and the interest on that printed dollar. This was the plan in 1913. Print money, and tax the taxpayer for every dollar printed.

Today, the taxpayer pays two taxes: One is direct taxes, and the other is inflation. And taxes and inflation are increasing.

This is why financial planners always advise, "Live below your means." You will have to live below your means just to pay your taxes and compensate for inflation.

This is also why there is no financial education in schools.

The government and the rich need people to pay the taxes and pay for inflation.

Be a Part of the Solution

Many Americans continue to believe that electing new political officials will solve the problems the United States faces. This is why we've seen a second "Tea Party" in America. In 1773, the first Tea Party was in Boston, a protest against the British government's taxation (without representation) in America. In 2010, a new Tea Party movement protested America's taxation of Americans.

In 2010, the British government announced that 500,000 government workers would lose their jobs. Those on welfare will also see their benefits cut.

In 2010, there were riots in the streets of Paris as the French protested increasing the retirement age from 60 to 62.

In 2010, Japan, a nation with a great education system that produces hardworking people who save a large percentage of their money, is the biggest debtor nation in the world, with their debt at 200 percent of GDP.

In 2010, China and Russia, once our mortal enemies, traded with each other, not in U.S. dollars, but in their respective currencies, the yuan and the ruble. This is no different than a banker refusing to lend money to a person with a poor credit score.

What does this all mean? It means the party is over. Santa's sleigh ride has ended.

It means capitalism is spreading to third-world nations.

This is good news if you are a capitalist. This is horrible news if you are a socialist, someone who expects the government to take care of you.

If you are a capitalist, you can be a part of the solution. If you are a socialist, you are the problem.

If you expect the government to solve your problems, you have a problem. The problem is that the governments of the world are broke.

Rather than be the problem, become part of the solution: Become a true capitalist, focusing on giving more to receive more. The days of expecting to be paid more for doing less are over.

Don't get me wrong. There is nothing wrong with having socialist ideals. We need people who care about others. But when you believe in a "free lunch," socialism turns to greed. And, as you know, the world is filled with greedy people, both socialists and capitalists.

Your true unfair advantage is to become financially educated so that you can become part of the solution rather than contribute to the problem.

Remember, a true capitalist focuses on doing more with less. That means better products at better prices. In a true environment of capitalism, prices come down as productivity goes up.

A Broken System

In my opinion, one of the bigger problems we face is our educational system. It is a system that still promotes earning more money for less work. Most teachers focus on job security and tenure, instead of how to teach more students with less of an investment.

Already, the best teachers are becoming rich because they are, first, better teachers and, second, using technology to teach more students.

The Chinese have arrived in the global marketplace and they know they must produce a better product at a better price, or unemployment will skyrocket as it has in the West. If the Western countries are to survive, we must get back to true capitalist values, the philosophy of doing more for less.

Unfortunately, the leaders in the West are primarily smart students who did well in school. The problem is that most smart students are trained in a socialist environment. Since most have limited financial or true business training, they leave school unprepared to lead in the real world.

Rather than promote prosperity, they promote austerity. Rather than promote production, they raise taxes, taxes that kill production.

The biggest problem with having leaders who are weak in terms of financial education is that it promotes corruption and greed.

Most of our brightest students are trained in a socialist environment, an environment that advocates taking from the rich to give to the poor. The problem is that the more we take from the rich and give to the poor, the more poor people we create. This pervasive attitude of wanting to be paid more for doing less must change.

So, going back to the original question...

FAQ
What is the greatest benefit from Rich Dad's financial education?

Short Answer
You can become a part of the solution.

Explanation
Your true unfair advantage is to use your financial education to be generous. Use your financial education to solve your own financial challenges and the financial challenges of others.

Remember: *Teaching* people to fish—rather than giving people fish—can create real change.

Unfortunately, rather than teach people to fish, our schools bring in people who sell fish. They bring in bankers and financial planners who sell fish rather than teach people to fish.

It disturbs me to hear financial planners, stockbrokers, real estate brokers, and insurance sales people dishing out sales pitches disguised as financial education. They are selling fish, a "sel-fish" approach to making money under the guise of education.

Rather than be selfish, and *sell fish* to naïve people, use your financial education to be generous.

Rather than use your unfair advantage to cheat and deceive the uneducated, use your financial education to teach, enlighten, and set people free.

Rather than use your unfair advantage to make only yourself richer, use your unfair financial education to enrich the lives of others.

One of our biggest problems is an antiquated education system that hangs on to the past and cannot see the future. It's an obsolete system that insists on preparing students for a world that is dead and dying.

In 2010, millions of people lost their jobs. Millions of people have lost their homes. Millions of people have lost their retirement savings. Millions of people lost because they were financially uneducated and relied on others to secure their financial futures.

Rather than allow this crisis to be a bad thing, use it as a motivator for something good. Teach yourself and teach others to think for themselves, rather than wait to be told what to do.

We truly are on the edge of a brave new world and a new world economy. This crisis is simply the end of an era. It is also the birth of a new era, a new economy.

The good news is that we are entering a new era of humanity, an era of unlimited abundance and opportunity. Advances in technology increase intelligence and reduce the cost of that intelligence. Technology decreases financial risk, reduces prices, brings wages down, and opens up worldwide markets. The good news is: Technology make it easier to be entrepreneurs.

The bad news is: Technology makes life harder for employees. That's why we're seeing rising unemployment as technology replaces workers, just as the automobile replaced horses.

Rather than going back to school only to focus on a higher-paying job, focus on looking for new ways to educate yourself. For the financially educated, it is a borderless world of abundance and opportunity.

Those who follow socialist and fascist dogma will continue to live in a world of scarcity... a world of lower wages, higher taxes and inflation, allowing their wealth to be stolen via fees and expenses by the very people to whom they entrust their wealth.

Conversely, life will grow easier for those who follow the three Laws of Compensation:

1. Give more to receive more.
2. Learn to give more, on the B and I side.
3. Leverage the power of compounding knowledge.

Not only will life be more abundant, but the government will offer you tax breaks, banks will loan you money to buy your assets, and Wall Street will raise money for entrepreneurs in the B quadrant.

Why are socialists and fascists so generous to capitalists? The answer is: They need capitalists. Without capitalists, socialists and fascists would be attacked by angry, hungry, out-of-work mobs.

Your financial education can give you an unfair advantage by preventing you from becoming a victim of the power play between the workers and the leaders.

Rather than be trapped between protesting workers and politicians, just focus on true capitalism.

Learn more so you can do more. Focus on doing more with less, and enriching the lives of others.

My Job… and Your Job

One of my heroes is Steve Jobs, co-founder and CEO of Apple, Inc. If not for Steve Jobs, I would never have written *Rich Dad Poor Dad* in 1997, or be using my iPhone to talk to the world.

Steve, a true entrepreneur and capitalist, made my life easier so that I could do my work of making other people's lives easier through financial education.

Your job is to use your unfair advantages to put the power of financial education to work in your life. First change yourself. Then change the world.

Special Thanks to...

Kim Kiyosaki

Ken McElroy

Garrett Sutton, Esq.

Andy Tanner

Tom Wheelwright, CPA

A Final Thought on Education

As a young boy, I hated school—but I loved learning.

I did not understand it at the time, but I now realize that school was training me to be an employee. And I wanted to be an entrepreneur. They are two very different worlds.

Over the years, I have come to respect the power of education. And I have learned that there are many types of education.

I've seen people grow old and bitter because they refuse to learn something new or change the way they think. We probably all know a few of these people.

What is Education?

I thank you for investing your time to read this book and hope that you have become a believer in the power of financial education.

If you have read any of my other books, you may know that I am not a great fan of traditional education. I did not like school, and my grades reflected my attitude. All I heard in school was, "If you don't get good grades, you won't get a good job." Well, I didn't want a job—and that was when I checked out of school.

My body may have been in the classroom, but my mind was always somewhere else. And maybe that was my unfair advantage.

About The Author
Robert Kiyosaki

Educational entrepreneur, creator of the *CASHFLOW* board game, founder of the financial education-based Rich Dad Company and author of *New York Times* bestsellers *Conspiracy of the Rich: The 8 New Rules of Money* and *Rich Dad Poor Dad*

Robert Kiyosaki is best known as the author of *Rich Dad Poor Dad*—the #1 personal finance book of all time—which has challenged and changed the way tens of millions of people around the world think about money. Rich Dad titles hold four of the top ten spots on Nielsen Bookscan List's Life-to-Date Sales from 2001-2008 alone. Robert has been featured on shows such as *Larry King Live, Oprah, The Doctors,* Bloomberg International Television and CNN.

With perspectives on money and investing that often contradict conventional wisdom, Robert has earned a reputation for straight talk, irreverence and courage. His point of view (that old advice—get a good job, save money, get out of debt, invest for the long term, and diversify—is obsolete advice) challenges the status quo. His assertion that "your house is not an asset" has stirred controversy, but has been proven to be accurate in our economy's current financial crisis.

In 2006, Robert teamed up with Donald Trump to co-author *Why We Want You To Be Rich – Two Men • One Message*. It debuted at #1 on *The New York Times* bestsellers list.

Robert was featured in *TIME* magazine's popular "10 Questions" column where Robert answered questions ranging from investing with few resources to the impact of education on one's financial success.

Robert's latest book, *Conspiracy of the Rich: The 8 New Rules of Money,* pioneered online book publishing as a free online interactive book with contributions from 1.1 million readers in over 167 countries. Frequent updates and postings appear on conspiracyoftherich.com

Get connected to the Rich Dad Global Community! Join for FREE!

You can expand your world and network in the league of Rich Dad in one single step. Join the Rich Dad Community FREE at **www.richdad.com** and globally expand your access to Robert, Kim and the Rich Dad Advisors. Connect, collaborate and play games with like-minded people who are committed to increasing their financial IQ – just like you!

Just for registering you will enjoy

- Inspiring discussion forums

- Listening to live web chats with Robert and Kim

- Exchanging ideas and information with others

- Challenging game play with others all around the world

- Learning first-hand about new releases from Robert and Kim

Rich Dad is committed to communicating with you through social media channels. Follow the inspiration threads on twitter, connect and participate in Rich Dad Facebook commentary and enjoy the benefits of the financially literate!

Visit www.facebook.com/
RobertKiyosaki
for what's on Robert's mind.

Visit **richdad.com** today and join the FREE
Rich Dad Community!